COMPANION
to the
BREVIARY

A Four-Week Psalter with Intercessions

Revised Edition
of the
New Companion to the Breviary

The Liturgy of the Hours with Inclusive Language

HOW TO USE THIS BOOK

This *Companion to the Breviary* contains the four-week psalter with intercessions. There is an index of psalms and a calendar indicates the proper week of the psalter to use for the years from 1997–2020.

Each **Psalm** follows a given antiphon. The **Antiphon** from the four-week Psalter or from the Season is generally prayed before and after the psalm. Three Psalms are used for each office. If two or more people are praying together, the verses of the psalms are alternated, i.e., one person or a group of persons prays a verse, then another person or group prays the following verse.

After the psalms, a **Reading** is usually read from the Scriptures of the current day or other spiritual reading for silent meditation or faith sharing among those praying together. The **Responsory** is begun by the leader and the group repeats the prayer as indicated by the parts printed in bold print.

After the antiphon for the **Canticle** is prayed, one may use the Canticle of Zechariah (on the last page) or the Canticle of Mary (on the inside back cover). Traditionally the Canticle of Zechariah is prayed in the morning and the Canticle of Mary is prayed in the evening, but the office chosen may dictate the preference of the group.

The **Intercessions** are begun by the leader and the group prays the response together. It is suggested that those praying add their own petitions after reading the intercessions given.

The **Prayer** can be prayed by the leader or in unison.

WEEK I

SUNDAY, EVENING PRAYER I

Ant 1 Let my prayer rise as incense before you.

Psalm 141:1-9

I call upon you, O God; make
  haste to help me;
give ear to my voice, when I call
  to you.
Let my prayer rise as incense
  before you,
and the lifting up of my hands as
  an evening sacrifice!

Set a guard over my mouth, O
  God,
keep watch over the door of my
  lips!
Do not incline my heart to evil,
that I not busy myself with
  wicked deeds
in company with those who work
  iniquity;
let me not partake of their
  dainties!

Let a good person strike or
  rebuke me in kindness,
but let the oil of wickedness
  never anoint my head;
for my prayer is constantly
  against wicked deeds.

When those who do evil are given
  over to those who condemn
  them,
then they shall learn that your
  word is true.—

***Glory to you, Source of all
Being, Eternal Word and Holy
Spirit,**

**As it was in the beginning is
now and will be forever. Amen.**

As a rock which one holds and
  shatters on the ground,
so shall their bones be strewn at
  the mouth of the grave.

But my eyes are turned toward
  you, O God;
in you I seek refuge; leave me not
  defenseless!
Keep me from the trap which evil
  lays before me,
and from the snares of my own
  wickedness. **Glory*...**

**Ant 2 You are my refuge, O
God; my portion in the land of
the living.**

Psalm 142

I cry out with my voice to you, O
  God,
with my voice I make supplication
  to you.
I pour out my complaints before
  you,
before you I place all my troubles.
When my spirit is faint, you, O
  God, know my way!

In the path where I walk
hidden traps surround me.
I look to the right and watch,
but no one takes notice of me;
no human refuge remains for me,
no one cares for my soul.

I cry out to you, O God;
I say, you are my refuge,
my portion in the land of the
  living.
Give heed to my cry;
for I am brought low, indeed!

Deliver me from those who would
  hurt me;
for they are too strong for me!
Bring me out of my distress,
that I may give thanks to your
  name!
Let your holy ones surround me;
for you will deal graciously with
  me. **Glory*...**

**Ant 3 Every tongue will
  proclaim the glory of God.**

Cant: Phil 2:6–11

Though he was in the form of
  God,
Jesus did not count equality with
  God
something to be grasped at.

But emptied himself—

taking the form of a slave,
being born in human likeness.

Being found in human estate,
he humbled himself and became
  obedient,
obediently accepting death,
even death on a cross!

Therefore God has highly exalted
  him
and bestowed on him the name
above every other name.

So that at the name of Jesus
every knee should bow,
in heaven, on the earth,
and under the earth,
and every tongue proclaim
to the glory of God:
Jesus Christ is Lord! **Glory*...**

READING

RESPONSORY

In love and thanksgiving, we praise you, Holy God. **—In love...**
Your name is written in our hearts; **—we praise...**
Glory to you, Source of all Being, Eternal Word and Holy Spirit.
  —In love...

CANTICLE OF MARY

Ant. Forever I will sing your praise.

INTERCESSIONS

Heaven and earth will pass away, but your word will remain, O
God;
  —let this promise of eternal life in you give meaning to
    our lives and energize us in your service.
You bless your people with a variety of talents, O God;
  —give us the courage to develop our gifts for your glory and
    the good of all.
Jesus, you foresaw the stark reality of the future, and you
encouraged your followers to have patience;

—help us to live the gospel so faithfully that our lives will be
a beacon of hope to others.
We are your children and you look upon us with love.
—help us to refrain from judging others negatively and to
temper justice with mercy.
Prayer is your invitation to realize our union with you;
—awaken us to your presence in us; teach us what it means
to pray always.

PRAYER: Most loving God, you pursue creation with your love
and rescue us with your mercy. Look upon us, your
people, this evening with tenderness and compassion.
Especially do we pray for all world leaders. May they all
find strength in your love and courage in your wisdom.
We ask this through the holy name of Jesus. Amen.

MORNING PRAYER

**Ant. 1 As morning breaks I
call upon your name, O God.**

Psalm 63:1–9

O God, you are my God, I long
for you;
my soul thirsts for you;
My body seeks for you
as in a dry and weary land
without water.
So I have looked upon you in
the sanctuary,
beholding your power and your
glory.

For your constant love is better
than life,
My lips will sing your praises.
So I will bless you as long as I
live;
I will lift up my hands and call
on your name.

My soul feasts on you and my
mouth praises you,
as I think of you upon my bed,-

and meditate on you in the
watches of the night;
for you have been my help,
In the shadow of your wings I
sing for joy.
My soul clings to you; your
hand upholds me.   **Glory*...**

**Ant. 2 Not fearing the flames
the three young men cried
out with one voice: Blessed
be God, (alleluia).**

Cant: Daniel 3:57–88, 56

All you works of God, praise
our God.
Praise and exalt God above all
forever.
All you angels, sing God's
praise,
you heavens and waters above.
Sun and moon, and stars of
heaven,
sing praise with the heavenly
hosts.

Every shower and dew, praise
our God.
Give praise all you winds.
Praise our God, you fire and
heat,
cold and chill—dew and rain.
Frost and chill, praise our God.
Praise God, ice and snow.
Nights and days, sing hymns of
praise,
light and darkness,
lightnings and clouds.

Let all the earth bless our God.
Praise and exalt God above all
forever.
Let all that grows from the
earth give praise,
together with mountains and
hills.
Give praise you springs,
you seas and rivers,
dolphins and all water
creatures.
Let birds of the air,
beasts wild and tame,
together with all living peoples,
praise and exalt God above all
forever.

O Israel praise our God.
Praise and exalt God above all
forever.
Give praise, you priests,
servants of the Most High,
spirits and souls of the just.
Holy ones of humble heart,
sing your hymns of praise.
Hananiah, Azariah, Mishael,
praise our God.
Praise and exalt God above all
forever.

Let us bless our God, Holy
Mystery,—

Source of All Being, Word, and
Spirit.
Let us praise and exalt God
above all forever.
Blessed are you, O God, in the
firmament of heaven.
Praiseworthy and glorious and
exalted above all forever.

**Ant. 3 Let the people of Zion
rejoice, (alleluia).**

Psalm 149

Sing a new song to our God,
Give praise in the assembly of
the faithful.
Let Israel be glad in its maker,
let Zion's heirs exult in the
Most High.
Let them praise God's name
with dancing,
and make music with timbrel
and harp.

For you take delight in your
people, O God.
You adorn the humble with
victory.
Let the faithful exult in their
glory,
in their rest, let them sing for
joy.
Let the praises of God be on
their lips
and two-edged swords in their
hands,

to wreak vengeance on all that
is wicked,
and chastisement on all
injustice;
to bind what is evil in chains
and oppression in fetters of
iron;—

to carry out the sentence pre-
ordained;—

this is glory for all God's
faithful ones. **Glory***...

READING

RESPONSORY

Christ, living word in our midst, hear our morning prayer.
   —Christ...
You are the light of the world; **—hear our...**
Glory to you, Source of all Being, Eternal Word and Holy Spirit.
   —Christ...

CANTICLE OF ZECHARIAH

Ant. Most gracious God, may you bless us all our days.

INTERCESSIONS

The earth is your masterpiece, O God, and you have made us its
stewards;
   —give us eyes to see your handiwork in every creature.
Creator is your name, and all that comes from your hand is
good;
   —cleanse our hearts and enlighten our minds that our
     choices may enhance and magnify your work in our world.
Your measuring rod is love;
   —give us a love that takes us out of and beyond ourselves.
Jesus, you know the strengths and weaknesses of the human
heart;
   —share with us your patience and compassion; remind us
     that another may carry a cross beyond our imagining.
Death is our last chance on earth to say yes to you, O God;
   —make us one with your will day by day.

PRAYER: O loving God we take delight in your people and all of
creation. Together we unite our hearts and voices to
sing your praise. Be with us this day and help us to
treat each other and all living creatures with respect
and appreciation. Grant this in the name of Jesus
who is our way, our truth, and our life. Amen.

DAYTIME PRAYER

Ant. 1 O God, to whom shall we go? You alone are our refuge.

Psalm 118

I

We give thanks to you, for you are good,
and your steadfast love endures forever.
Let the descendants of Israel say:
"Your steadfast love endures forever."
Let the descendants of Aaron say:
"Your steadfast love endures forever."
Let those who fear you say:
"Your steadfast love endures forever."

In my distress, I called to you;
you answered me and set me free.
With you at my side I do not fear.
What can anyone do against me?
You are at my side to help me:
I shall withstand all evildoers.

It is better to take refuge in you,
than to trust in people:
it is better to take refuge in you
than to trust in our leaders.
    Glory*...

Ant. 2 God's holy hand has raised me up, (alleluia).

II

All wickedness surrounded me;
in your name I crushed it.
It surrounded me, surrounded me
on every side;
in your name I cut it off.
It surrounded me like bees;
it blazed like a fire among thorns.
In your name I crushed it.

I was pushed hard, and was falling
but you came to help me.
You are my strength and my song;
you are my salvation.

O God, you have triumphed;
your reign is exalted.
You have triumphed over all;
I shall not die, I shall live
and recount your wondrous deeds.
You have chastened me sorely,
but have not given me over to
    death. **Glory*...**

Ant. 3 Our God has let the light of the Most High to shine upon us, (alleluia).

III

Open to me the gates of justice,
that I may enter and give thanks.
This is your gate, O God;
the just shall enter through it.
I thank you for you have answered
    me
you alone are my salvation.

The stone which the builders
    rejected
has become the cornerstone.
This is your doing, O God,
it is marvelous in our eyes.
This is the day which you have
    made;
let us rejoice and be glad in it.

Save us, we beseech you, O God!
O God, grant us success.
Blessed are those who enter
in your holy name.
For you O God, are our God,
and you have given us light.

Let us go forward in procession
    with branches,—

up to your holy altar.
You are my God, I thank you.
You are my God, I praise you.—

We give thanks to you for you are good;
and your steadfast love endures forever. **Glory*...**

PRAYER: Most holy God, we rejoice in your gift of life as shared with us in the paschal mystery. On this day of remembrance, help us to enter more deeply into the mystery of your life lived among us, your people. We ask this in the name of Jesus, who lived as one of us, and through your Spirit who enlivens us. Amen.

EVENING PRAYER II

Ant. 1 God's reign will last forever.
Psalm 110:1-5, 7

God's revelation to the Anointed One:
"Sit at my side:
till I put injustice beneath your feet."

God will send forth from Zion
your scepter of power:
rule in the midst of your foes.

Your people will give themselves freely
on the day you lead your host
upon the holy mountains.
From the womb of the morning
your your youth will come like dew.

God has sworn an oath that will not be changed.
"You are a priest forever,
after the order of Melchizedek."

The Anointed standing at your side,
will shatter rulers on the day of wrath.

Drinking from your streams by the wayside
shall the Chosen One be refreshed. **Glory*...**

Ant. 2 Tremble, O earth, at the presence of your God.
Psalm 114

When Israel went forth from Egypt,
Jacob's heirs from an alien people,
Judah became God's sanctuary,
Israel, the dominion of the Most High.

The sea looked and fled,
Jordan turned back on its course.
The mountains skipped like rams,
the hills like yearling lambs.

What ails you, O sea, that you flee?
O Jordan, that you turn back?
Mountains, that you skip like rams,
hills, like yearling lambs?

Tremble, O earth, at the
presence of God,
at the presence of the God of
your ancestors,
who turns the rock into a pool,
the flint into a spring of water.
Glory...

**Ant. 3 All power is yours, O
God, creator of all.**
Cant: Rev 19:1, 5–7

Salvation, glory, and power
belong to you,
your judgments are honest and
true.

All of us, your servants, sing
praise to you,
we worship you reverently, both
great and small.

You, our almighty God, are
Creator of heaven and earth.
Let us rejoice and exult, and
give you glory.

The wedding feast of the Lamb
has begun,
And the bride has made herself
ready. **Glory*...**

READING

RESPONSORY

Incline my heart to praise your goodness all the days of my life.
—**Incline...**
For my prayer is always before you; —**all the...**
Glory to you, Source of all Being, Eternal Word and Holy Spirit.
—**Incline...**

CANTICLE OF MARY

Ant. You fill us with goodness and mercy.

INTERCESSIONS

Spirit of God, you lead each of us in a direction that is life-giving
and fruitful;
—help us to silence all that would deafen us to your call.
As the possibilities of science continue to expand;
—remind us of our creaturehood and give us humble hearts.
Life is your gift to us, O God, and your love for us gives meaning
to your gift;
—show yourself to those who are tempted to despair.
Jesus, you knew the cares of family life;
—encourage and strengthen heads of families who face the
special challenges of our culture.
Jesus you healed on the Sabbath and were persecuted for it;
—be with our present day prophets who make unpopular
decisions for the cause of justice and truth.

PRAYER: You, O God, are our place of refuge; you continue to call us forth to be your people in a world of division and distress. Help us to be people of faith, joy, and love in the midst of chaos. This we ask through the intercession of Jesus, Mary, and Joseph, who imaged community in a captive and oppressed land. Amen.

MONDAY

MORNING PRAYER

Ant 1 Give heed to my words, O God, and listen to my morning prayer.

Psalm 5:1–9, 11–12

Give ear to my words, O God,
give heed to my groaning.
Attend to the sound of my cry,
O God, Most High.

For it is you to whom I pray.
In the morning you hear my voice;
I prepare a sacrifice for you,
watching and waiting.

You are not a God delighting in evil;
no sinner is your companion.
The boastful may not stand before you,
before your holy face.

You hate all that is evil;
you destroy all that is false.
The deceitful and the bloodthirsty
you chastise, O God.

But I through the abundance of your love
will enter your holy house.
I will worship at your holy temple,
filled with awe.

Lead me, O God, in your justice;
there are those who seek to seduce me,—

make clear your way before me.

For there is no truth in their mouth,
their heart is destruction,
their throat is a wide-open grave,
all flattery their speech.

Let all be glad who take refuge in you,
forever sing out their joy.
Shelter those who love your name;
May they ever exult in you.

For you it is who bless the just;
you cover them with favor,
as with a shield. **Glory***...

Ant. 2 We sing your praises from generation to generation.

Cant: 1 Chron 9:10b–13

Blessed may you be,
O God of Israel,
from eternity to eternity.

Yours, O God, are grandeur and power,
majesty, splendor, and glory.

For all in heaven and on earth is yours;
yours, O God, is the sovereignty;
you are exalted as head over all.

Riches and honor are from you;—

you have dominion over all.
In your hands are power and
  might;
it is yours to give grandeur and
  strength to all.

Therefore, our God, we give you
  thanks
and we praise the majesty of
  your name. **Glory*...**

**Ant. 3 You are the Alpha and
the Omega, the first and the
last, the beginning and the
end.**

Psalm 29

O give to God, you heavenly
  beings,
give to God glory and power;
give glory to God's holy name.
Worship your God in holy array.

For God's voice is heard on the
  waters,—

thundering on many waters;
the voice of God is powerful,
God's voice, full of splendor.

Your voice shatters the cedars,
it shatters the cedars of Lebanon;
you make Lebanon skip like a calf
and Sirion like a young wild ox.

Your voice, O God flashes flames
  of fire.
Your voice shakes the wilderness
  of Kadesh;
it makes the oak trees whirl,
and strips the forests bare.

The God of glory thunders!
In your temple all cry: "Glory!"
You sit enthroned over the flood;
you sit, our sovereign forever.

May you give strength to your
  people,
and bless your people with peace.
  Glory*...

READING

RESPONSORY

Shelter us, O God, in the safety of your dwelling place. **—Shelter...**
Your name is forever blessed; **—in the**...
Glory to you, Source of all Being, Eternal Word and Holy Spirit.
  —Shelter...

CANTICLE OF ZECHARIAH

Ant. You are faithful to your word, forever.

INTERCESSIONS

O God, you bow to our weakness and need;
  —deliver us from temptation and guide us in the way of truth.
Your Spirit prays in us for what we know not how to ask;
  —let that same Spirit draw us to a maturity worthy of you.
Jesus, you drew your disciples to yourself and taught them
eternal truths;

—bless the young people who must live in our streets,
    jobless and tempted to crime and despair.
Our minds and hearts are pulled in many directions;
    —let the words of your gospel unify and direct our lives.
The sick and the poor were drawn to you;
    —help us to find ways to care for all who are terminally ill.

PRAYER: O Holy God, you continue to bless us with your gifts of
    creation. We give thanks to you for your kindness to
    your people, and we take delight in the gifts we share
    to bring about the fullness of your life in our world. All
    praise to you, Most Blessed Trinity, living in us and
    among us through all generations. Amen.

DAYTIME PRAYER

**Ant. 1 Teach us to love you and
our neighbor, so as to fulfill
your law.**
Psalm 19:7–14

Your law, O God, is perfect,
reviving the soul.
Your testimony is to be trusted,
making the simple wise.

Your precepts are right,
rejoicing the heart.
Your command is pure,
giving light to the eyes.

The fear of God is holy,
enduring forever.
God's ordinances are true,
and all of them just.

More to be desired are they than
  gold,
more than the purest gold,
and sweeter are they than honey,
than drippings from the comb.

By them your servant finds
  instruction;
great reward is in their keeping.
But who can detect all one's
  errors?—

From hidden faults acquit me.

Restrain me from presumptuous
  sins,
let them not have rule over me!
Then shall I be blameless,
and clean from serious sin.

Let the words of my mouth,
the thoughts of my heart,
be acceptable in your sight,
O God, my rock and my
  redeemer. **Glory*...**

**Ant. 2 Judge me, O God,
according to your law.**
Psalm 7
I

O God, in you I take refuge;
Save me from my pursuers and
  rescue me,
lest they tear me to pieces like a
  lion,
dragging me off with none to
  rescue me.

O God, if I have done this,
if my hands have done wrong,
if I have paid my friend with evil
or plundered without cause,—

then let my foes pursue me and
  seize me,
let them trample my life to the
  ground
and lay my soul in the dust.

Let the assembly of nations
  gather round you,
taking your seat above them on
  high.
For you, O God, are judge of the
  peoples.

Judge me, O God, according to
  my justice,
and according to the integrity
  that is mine.
Put an end to the evil of the
  wicked;
and make the just stand firm,
you who test the mind and heart,
you, our most just God!
  Glory*...

**Ant. 3 Search me, O God, and
know my heart; cleanse me
from all sin.**

II

God is the shield that protects
  me,
who saves the upright of heart.—

God is a just judge
slow to anger;
challenging the wicked every day,
those who are slow to repent.

God sharpens the sword,
bends the bow that is strung,
prepares deadly weapons for
  wickedness,
and barbs the arrows with fire.
Behold those who are pregnant
  with malice,
who conceive evil and bring forth
  lies.

They dig a pitfall, dig it deep;
and fall into the trap they have
  made.
Their malice will recoil on
  themselves;
on their own heads their violence
  will fall.

I will give thanks to you, God,
for your justice;
and will sing to your name,
  O Most High. **Glory*...**

PRAYER: As we pause to remember your fidelity to us, O Source
of Life, continue to abide with us this day. We give
thanks for all people working for justice and peace, and
we ask you, O God, to come in power to give your
people courage and strength. We ask this through the
intercession of Jesus and all who have given their lives
in the cause of justice. Amen.

EVENING PRAYER

Ant. 1 Teach us how to act justly, and to walk humbly with one another.
Psalm 11

In God I have taken my refuge.
How can you say to my soul:
"Fly like a bird to the mountains.

See the wicked bending the bow;
they have fitted their arrows on
the string
to shoot the upright in the dark.
If the foundations are destroyed,
what can the righteous do?"

But you are in your holy temple,
you, whose throne is in heaven.
Your eyes look down on the
world;
your gaze tests mortal flesh.

God tests the just and the
wicked,
scorned by the lovers of violence.
God will chastise those who do
evil;
a scorching wind shall be their
lot.

You are just and love justice;
the upright shall behold your
face. **Glory*...**

Ant. 2 Create in me an upright spirit that I may serve you in others.
Psalm 15

Who shall visit in your tent,
and dwell on your holy
mountain?

They who walk blamelessly,
and do what is right,
who speak the truth from their
hearts;—

and do not slander with their
tongues;

they who do no wrong to each
other,
nor cast reproaches on their
neighbors,
who pray the godless to repent,
and honor those who fear the
Most High;

they who keep their pledge, come
what may;
who take no profit from injustice,
nor accept bribes against the
innocent.
Such as these will stand firm
forever. **Glory*...**

Ant. 3 We are your people, chosen before the foundation of the world.
Cant: Ephesians 1:3–10

Praised be the God
of our Lord Jesus Christ,
who has blessed us in Christ
with every spiritual blessing in
the heavens.

God chose us in him
before the foundation of the
world,
that we should be holy
and blameless in God's sight.

We have been predestined
to be God's children through
Jesus Christ,
such was the purpose of God's
will,
that all might praise the glorious
favor
bestowed on us in Christ.

In Christ and through his blood,
we have redemption,
the forgiveness of our sins,
according to the riches of God's
  grace lavished upon us.

For God has made known to us
in all wisdom and insight,—

the mystery of the plan set forth
  in Christ.

A plan to be carried out in Christ,
in the fullness of time,
to unite all things in Christ,
things in heaven and things on
  earth. **Glory*...**

READING

RESPONSORY

Look upon us graciously, O God, and have mercy on us. **—Look...**
For you are our source of love; **—have**...
Glory to you, Source of all Being, Eternal Word and Holy Spirit.
    —Look...

CANTICLE OF MARY

Ant. I long for you, God of my life.

INTERCESSIONS

Jesus, you loved the land of your birth;
    —bless all nations torn by war and division.
You were filled with the Holy Spirit, the very Wisdom of God;
    —enlighten and guide all who labor to discover insights
        toward our spiritual and physical healing and growth.
Many believed in you because of your miracles;
    —let our love for you and for one another be the sign that
        draws others to you.
You welcomed outcasts and dined with them;
    —teach us how to reverently minister to those who are
        rejected today.
Your gospel is a call to life;
    —bring its message of peace to those who are dying.

PRAYER: Most loving God, you love justice. Help us to be open
            to your ways of mercy, compassion, and truth that we
            may call forth in ourselves and in one another your
            ways of wisdom and truth. We ask this through the
            Holy Spirit of Wisdom living in you through all eternity.
            Amen.

TUESDAY
MORNING PRAYER

**Ant. 1 Blessed are the pure of
heart, for they shall see God.**
Psalm 24

Yours is the earth and its fullness,
the world and all who dwell there;
for you have founded it upon the
seas,
and established it upon the rivers.

Who shall climb your mountain, O
God?
Who shall stand in your holy
place?
Those with clean hands and pure
hearts,
who do not desire what is vain,
who have not sworn so as to
deceive their neighbors.

They shall receive blessings from
the Most High,
and reward from the God who
saves them.
Such are those who seek after the
Holy One;
who seek the face of the God of
their ancestors.

O gates, lift up your heads;
grow higher, ancient doors.
Let enter the God of glory!

Who is this God of glory?
The One who is mighty and
valiant,
valiant against all injustice.

O gates, lift up your heads;
grow higher, ancient doors.
Let enter the God of glory!

Who is this God of glory?
You, the God of hosts,
You, O God, are the God of glory.
   Glory*...

**Ant. 2 Turn to me, O God, and
show me your face.**

Cant: Tobit 13:1b–8

Blessed be God who lives forever,
whose realm lasts for all ages.

For you scourge, O God, and then
have mercy;
you cast down to the depths of the
nether world,
and bring up from the great abyss.
No one can escape your hand.

Praise God, you Israelites, before
the Gentiles,
for though you are scattered
among them,
you have seen God's greatness
even there.

Exalt God before every living
being,
because you, O God, are the Most
High,
our God forever and ever.

God has scourged you for your
iniquities,
but will again have mercy on you
all.
Gathering you from all the
Gentiles
among whom you have been
scattered.

When you turn back to God with
all your heart,
to do only what is right,
then God will turn back to you,
God's face will no longer be
hidden.

So now consider what has been
done for you,—

and give praise with full voice.
Bless the God of righteousness,
and exalt the Ruler of the ages.

In the land of my exile I praise
 you, O God,
and show your power and majesty
 to a sinful nation.
"Turn back, you sinners! do what
 is right:
perhaps God may look with favor
 upon you
and show you mercy.

As for me, I exult in my God,
and my spirit rejoices.
Let all speak of God's majesty,
and sing God's praises in
 Jerusalem." **Glory*...**

**Ant. 3 Blessed are those who
 hear your word and keep it.
 Psalm 33**

Rejoice in God, O you just;
praise is fitting for loyal hearts.
We give thanks to you with the
 lyre,
make melody with ten-stringed
 harps.
Let us sing a song that is new,
and play skillfully, full of gladness.

For your words, O God are faithful
and all your works to be trusted.
You love justice and
 righteousness,
and fill the earth with your
 steadfast love.

By your word the heavens were
 made,
by the breath of your mouth all
 the stars.
You gather the waters of the
 oceans;—

you store up the depths of the
 seas.

Let all the earth fear you, O God,
all who live in the world, stand in
 wonder.
For you spoke; and it came to be.
You commanded; it sprang into
 being.

You frustrate the designs of the
 nations,
you upset the plans of the peoples.
Your own designs stand forever,
the plans of your heart to all
 generations.

Happy are they whose God you
 are,
the peoples you have chosen for
 your heritage.
From the heavens you look forth,
and see all the peoples of the
 earth.

From the place where you dwell
 you gaze
on all the dwellers of this earth,
you who fashion the hearts of
 them all
and observe all their deeds.

Rulers are not saved by their
 armies,
nor leaders preserved by their
 strength.
A vain hope for safety are our
 weapons;
despite their power they cannot
 save.

Look on those who reverence you,
on those who hope in your love,
to deliver their souls from death,
and keep them alive in famine.

Our souls are waiting for you;
you are our help and our shield.—

In you do our hearts find joy; we trust in your holy name.

Let your love be upon us, O God, as we place all our hope in you.
Glory*...

READING

RESPONSORY

You call us each by name, for we are blessed in you. **—You call...**
Faithful to your promise; **—for we are...**
Glory to you, Source of all Being, Eternal Word and Holy Spirit.
—You call...

CANTICLE OF ZECHARIAH

Ant. You are our God and holy is your name.

INTERCESSIONS

Jesus, you enabled your disciples to hear your call and to follow you;
—enable all Christians to discern the promptings of your Spirit and to respond wholeheartedly.
Through your death and rising, we have become your body; your Spirit lives on in us;
—awaken us to our responsibility as your people; let us meet each other with openness and good will.
Your apostle Paul prayed for an end to division within his community;
—teach us positive ways to heal our differences and to cultivate peace of mind for ourselves and our children.
Jesus, our Savior, you were taught and nourished by the words of Scripture;
—may our hearing of the word of God today help us to bring quality of life to those who are imprisoned, the oppressed, and the disabled.
O God, time after time you spoke to your people and drew them to conversion of heart;
—grant us the ability to read the signs of the times, that we may hear your call to a change of heart as individuals and as a people.

PRAYER: Most compassionate God, touch our hearts this morning with your mercy and love. Help us to be a source of love and light to those who are suffering this day. May all who die today experience the joy of being in your presence. Grant this through the intercession of all who suffered persecution for the sake of justice. Amen.

DAYTIME PRAYER

Ant. 1 The just shall praise you with upright hearts.
Psalm 119:1–8

Blessed are they whose way is
  blameless,
who follow your law, O God!
Blessed are they who do your will,
who seek you with all their hearts,
who never do anything wrong,
but walk in your ways.

You have laid down your precepts
to be diligently kept.
O that my ways may be firm
in obeying your statutes.
Then I shall not be put to shame
as I heed your commands.

I will praise you with an upright
  heart
as I learn your decrees.
I will obey your statutes;
do not forsake me.   **Glory*...**

Ant. 2 My heart rejoices in your saving grace, O God.
Psalm 13

How long, O God? Will you forget
  me forever?
How long will you hide your face?
How long must I bear pain in my
  soul,
and sorrow in my heart day and
  night?—

How long shall my oppressors
  prevail?

Look at me, answer me, my God!
Lighten my eyes lest I sleep the
  sleep of death,
lest my oppressors say: "I have
  overcome you";
lest they rejoice to see me shaken.

As for me, I trust in your merciful
  love.
My heart rejoices in your
  salvation;
I will sing to you for your
  goodness,
because you are gracious to me.
    Glory*...

Ant. 3 Give us your wisdom that we may follow your way.
Psalm 14

Fools say in their hearts:
"There is no God!"
They are corrupt, their deeds,
  depraved;
there are none that do good.

But you look down from heaven,
upon the peoples of the earth,
to see if any are wise,
if any seek God.

All seem to have gone astray,
depraved, every one;
there are none that do good,
no, not even one.

Do evildoers have no knowledge?
They eat up God's people
as though they were eating bread;
do they never call upon the Most
High God?

There they shall be in great terror,
for God is with the just.
You may mock the hope of the
poor,—

but their refuge is the Most High
God.

O that Israel's salvation might
come from Zion!
When God delivers the people from
bondage,
then Jacob shall rejoice and Israel
be glad. **Glory*...**

PRAYER: Gentle God, you remind us that you are our faithful
friend, and that you will deliver us from bondage.
Look upon us, your people, and deliver us from the
chains that keep us from the fullness of life. We pray
this in love and confidence in Jesus' name. Amen.

EVENING PRAYER

**Ant. 1 Only in you, O God, will
my soul be at rest.**

Psalm 20

May God answer in time of
trouble!
May the name of our God protect
you.

Send your help, O God, from your
sanctuary,
and give your support from Zion.
May you remember all our
offerings
and receive our sacrifice with
favor.

May you give us our heart's desire
and fulfill every one of our plans.
May we ring out our joy at your
victory
and rejoice in your name, O God.
May you grant all our prayers.

Now I know that you, O God,
will give victory to your anointed;
you will reply from your holy
heaven—

with the help of your hand.

Some trust in chariots or horses,
but we trust in your holy name.
They will collapse and fall,
but we shall rise and stand firm.

Give victory to your Anointed,
give answer on the day we call.
Glory*...

**Ant. 2 To know you, O God, is
to possess eternal life.**

Psalm 21:2-8, 14

O God, your strength gives joy to
your people;
how your saving help makes them
glad!
You have granted them the desire
of their hearts;
you have not refused the prayer of
their lips.

You came to meet them with
goodly blessings,
you have set blessings on their
heads.—

They asked you for life and this
you have given,
length of days forever and ever.

Your saving help has given them
glory.
Splendor you bestow upon them.
You grant your blessings to them
forever.
You gladden them with the joy of
your presence.

They put their trust in you:
through your steadfast love, they
shall stand firm.
O God, we exult in your strength;
we shall sing and praise your
goodness. **Glory*...**

**Ant. 3 O God, you have made us
in your own image.**
Cant: Rev 4:11, 5:9, 10, 12

Worthy are you, O God, our
God,—

to receive glory and honor and
power.

For you have created all things;
by your will they came to be and
were made.

Worthy are you to take the scroll
and to open its seals,

For you were slain, and by your
blood,
you purchased for God
saints of every race and tongue,
of every people and nation.

You have made of them a kindom,
and priests to serve our God,
and they shall reign on the earth.

Worthy is the Lamb who was slain
to receive power and riches,
wisdom and strength,
honor and glory and praise.
Glory*...

READING

RESPONSORY

In you, Word of God, I place my trust and love.—**In you...**
For you are our redeemer; —**I place...**
Glory to you, Source of all Being, Eternal Word and Holy Spirit.
—**In you...**

CANTICLE OF MARY

Ant. My soul will sing your praises.

INTERCESSIONS

O God, you are ever calling us to greater freedom, to walk in the
light, to grow, and to deepen our lives;
—give us the desire and the courage to respond fully to your
goodness; make our lives pleasing to you.
Your compassion is boundless; you uphold your gift of freedom to
us;

—deliver us from timidity and all that would keep us from
    turning to you.
Jesus, you respected those who worked with their hands; some
became your disciples;
    —preserve the dignity of those who work for others; deliver
      them from harassment of any kind.
You prayed with your people and read to them from the
Scriptures;
    —may all who lend their gifts to liturgical service enrich
      our lives and be blessed in their sharing.
You promised to be with us till the end of time;
    —may the words of your gospel keep hope alive in our hearts.

PRAYER: At the close of our day, we turn to you, our God, and
        with hearts of gratitude, we ask you to remember our
        deeds of goodness and to have mercy upon our
        shortcomings. May all who have died this day find
        peace in you and may all the sorrowing find comfort in
        those around them and in your compassionate heart.
        We ask this mindful of your mercy and forgiveness.
        Amen.

WEDNESDAY

MORNING PRAYER

**Ant 1 You are the light of the
    world.**

Psalm 36

Sin speaks to the wicked
in the depths of their hearts.
There is no fear of God
before their eyes.

They so flatter themselves in their
  own eyes
that they know not their own
  guilt.
In their mouths are mischief and
  deceit.
They no longer act wisely or good.

They plot the defeat of goodness
as they lie on their beds.—

They set their feet on evil ways,
and do not spurn what is evil.

But your steadfast love extends to
  the heavens,
your faithfulness to the skies.
Your justice is like the mountain,
your judgments like the great
  deep.

To both human and beast you
  give salvation.
How precious is your love.
The children of this earth
take refuge in the shadow of your
  wings.

They feast on the riches of your
  house;—

and drink from the stream of your
  delight.
In you is the fountain of life
and in your light we see light.

Keep on loving those who know
  you,
giving salvation to upright hearts.
Let the foot of the proud not
  crush me
nor the hand of the wicked drive
  me away.

There the evildoers lie prostrate!
Thrust down, they are unable to
  rise. **Glory*...**

**Ant. 2 Let all creation bow
  down before you.**
  Cant: Judith 16:1, 13–15

Strike up the instruments,
a song to my God with timbrels,
chant to the Most High with
  cymbals.
Sing a new song,
exalt and acclaim God's name.

A new hymn I will sing to you.
O God, great are you and
  glorious,
wonderful in power and
  unsurpassable.

Let your every creature serve you;
for you spoke, and they were
  made,
you sent forth your spirit, and
  they were created;
no one can resist your word.

The mountains to their bases,
  and the seas, are shaken;—

READING

RESPONSORY

the rocks, like wax, melt before
  your glance.
But to those who fear you,
  you are very merciful. **Glory*...**

**Ant. 3 We sing praise to you,
Most High.**

Psalm 47

Clap your hands, all you peoples,
shout to God with songs of joy!
For the Most High we must fear,
great ruler over all the earth!

O God, you subdue evil
  oppression,
and challenge unjust nations.
You chose our heritage for us,
gave it to us out of love.

You go up with shouts of joy;
O God, with trumpet blast.
We sing praise to you, sing
  praise,
sing praise to you, Most High.

For your realm is all the earth.
We sing to you our hymns of
  praise!
Your reign is over all the nations;
Over all the peoples of this earth.

The leaders of the peoples gather
with the people of Abraham's
  God.
May all leaders of the earth pay
  heed,
to God who reigns over all.
  Glory*...

Living source of light and wisdom, be with us always. **—Living...**
In you we find new life; **—be with...**

Glory to you, Source of all Being, Eternal Word and Holy Spirit.
—**Living...**

CANTICLE OF ZECHARIAH

Ant. You are faithful to your promise, God of all the ages.

INTERCESSIONS

O God, you know our coming and our going, and you bless our every effort to live justly;
—help us to remember your faithfulness and that our inspiration and strength is your gift.
You have power over all that you have created;
—enable warring nations to redeem the wounds of the past and to discover creative ways to peace.
Jesus, you were rejected by your own people;
—direct each of us to a milieu that is receptive of our gifts.
Love is patient and kind, but a stressful world can thin our resources;
—have mercy on parents who are overworked and fearful; guide and protect teen-agers who run away from home.
Mindful that you call us to be a light in darkness, we pray;
—be with us in our poverty and need.

PRAYER: O God, source of our light, you are ever with us to reveal the way of truth and justice. Be with us this day as we struggle to ease the burdens of our sisters and brothers. We ask this in Jesus who is our way, our truth, and our life. Amen.

DAYTIME PRAYER

Ant. 1 Your law is written on my heart.
Psalm 119:9–16

How shall the young remain sinless?
By living according to your word.
I have sought you with all my heart;
let me not stray from your commands.

I carry your word in my heart lest I sin against you.
Blessed are you, O God;
teach me your statutes.

With my lips I have recounted all the decrees of your mouth.
I delight to do your will as though all riches were mine.

I will meditate on your precepts and fix my eyes on your ways.—

I will delight in your statutes;
I will not forget your word.
    Glory*...

**Ant. 2 You are a light to my
eyes, a lamp for my feet.**

Psalm 17

O God, hear a cause that is just,
attend to my cry.
Give ear to my prayer
from lips free of deceit.

If you should try my heart
or visit me by night;
if you should test me,
you will find no deceit in me;
my tongue has not deceived.

Because of the word of your
  mouth
I have avoided the ways of the
  violent.
My steps have held fast to your
  paths,
my feet have not slipped.

I call upon you, for you will hear
  me.
Turn your ear to me; hear my
  words.
Show your steadfast love,
to all who seek refuge
in the shelter of your hand.

Keep me as the apple of your eye.
Hide me in the shadow of your
  wings—

from the wicked who seek to
  destroy. **Glory*...**

**Ant. 3 You are my portion, the
God of my life.**

II

They close their hearts to pity;
with their mouths they speak
  arrogantly.
They track me down, surrounding
  me;
setting their eyes to cast me to
  the ground
as though they were a lion eager
  to tear,
as a young lion lurking in
  ambush.

Arise, O God, confront them,
  strike them down!
Deliver my life from the wicked;
by your hand, O God, rescue me
  from evildoers,
from those whose portion is of
  this world.

May they be filled from the
  abundance of your storehouse;
may their children have more
  than enough;
may their wealth extend to their
  offspring.

As for me, in my justice I shall
  see your face;
when I awake, I shall be filled
  with the sight of your glory.
    Glory*...

PRAYER: God of wisdom, enlighten us with your spirit that we
may work to bring about your love and justice within
our hearts and in the hearts of all your people.
Strengthen us with insight to be faithful to your word
revealed among us. Grant this through the
intercessions of all those who faithfully heard your
word and kept it. Amen.

EVENING PRAYER

Ant. 1 You are my dwelling place, in you I take my rest.

Psalm 27

O God, you are my light and my
  help;
whom shall I fear?
You are the stronghold of my life;
before whom shall I be afraid?

When evildoers assail me
uttering slanders against me,
it is they, my enemies and foes,
who shall stumble and fall.

Though an army encamp against
  me
my heart shall not fear.
Though war break out against me
yet will I trust.

One thing I have asked of you,
for this will I seek,
that I may dwell in your holy
  house
all the days of my life,
to behold the beauty of your
  countenance
and the holiness of your temple.

In your shelter you will hide me
in the day of trouble;
you will conceal me under the
  cover of your tent,
you will set me high upon a rock.

And now my head shall be raised
above my foes who surround me;
and I will offer in your tent
sacrifices with songs of joy.
I will sing and make music to my
  God. **Glory*...**

Ant. 2 It is you, O God that I seek.

II

Hear my voice when I cry aloud,
be gracious to me and give
  answer!
You say to me: "Seek my face,
Seek the face of your God."

"Your face, O God, I do seek."
Hide not your face from me.
Do not dismiss me in anger;
you have been my help.

Do not cast me off or forsake me,
O God, my help!
Though father and mother
  forsake me,
You, O God, will receive me.

Teach me your way, O God;
lead me on a level path.
Give me not up to the will of
  evildoers;
who bear false witness and
  breathe out violence.

I believe I shall see your goodness
in the land of the living.
Hope in God, be strong and take
  heart.
Hope in God, the Most High!
  Glory*...

Ant. 3 Jesus is the image of the invisible God.

Cant: Colossians 1:12–20

Let us give thanks to God
for having made us worthy
to share the inheritance of the
  saints in light.

God has delivered us
from the power of darkness
and transferred us
into the kindom of God's beloved
Son, Jesus,
in whom we have redemption,
the forgiveness of our sins.

Jesus is the image of the invisible
God,
the first-born of all creation;
in him all things were created,
in heaven and on earth,
things visible and invisible.

All things were created through
him;
all were created for him.—

He is before all else that is.
In him all things hold together.

He is the head of the body, the
church!
He is the beginning,
the firstborn from the dead,
that in everything, he might be
above all others.

In him all the fullness of God was
pleased to dwell,
and through him, to reconcile all
things to himself,
whether on earth or in heaven,
making peace by the blood of his
cross. **Glory*...**

READING

RESPONSORY

Hold me gently, O God, in the palm of your hand. **—Hold...**
In you I find my rest; **—in the...**
Glory to you, Source of all Being, Eternal Word and Holy Spirit.
    —Hold...

CANTICLE OF MARY

**Ant. You have done great things for us and holy is your
    name.**

INTERCESSIONS

Everything is a gift;
    —O God, make us good stewards of what we have, and grant
    us the help we need to be a sign of your kindom.
You created our bodies as temples of the Holy Spirit;
    —send your healing to victims of rape, incest, and every
    form of violence that destroys and deforms.
You call each one of us to be holy;
    —help us to reflect the divine imprint of your creativity in our
    lives.
You bless those who bear insult and persecution;
    —give wise advocates to those who are falsely accused; make
    us humble and just in our speech.

In the many voices that cry out for attention, help us to recognize you and to pray;
—"Speak, O God, for your servant is listening."

PRAYER: In the evening we come to you, O God, to thank you for the blessings of this day. May we be ever mindful of your love in the midst of life's joys and burdens, and may all your people experience your peace this night. This we ask placing ourselves in your care, Most Blessed Trinity. Amen.

THURSDAY

MORNING PRAYER

Ant. 1 In the early hours of the morning, my heart will sing your praise.
Psalm 57

Have mercy on me, have mercy,
for in you my soul takes refuge.
In the shadow of your wings I take refuge
till the storms of destruction pass by.

I cry to God the Most High,
to God who has always been my help.
May you send from heaven and save me
and shame those who trample upon me.
O God, send your truth and your love.

My soul lies down among lions,
who greedily devour the peoples of the earth.
Their teeth are spears and arrows,
their tongues a sharpened sword.

Be exalted, O God, above the heavens;
let your glory be over all the earth!

They laid a snare for my steps,
my soul was bowed down.
They dug a pit in my path
but they fell in it themselves.

My heart is steadfast, O God,
my heart is steadfast.
I will sing and make melody!
Awake, my soul,
awake, lyre and harp!
I will awake the dawn!

I will give thanks to you among the peoples,
I will praise you among the nations
for your love reaches to the heavens
your faithfulness to the skies.

Be exalted, O God, above the heavens!
let your glory be over all the earth!
Glory*...

Ant. 2 You are the bread of life; you are the cup of salvation.
Cant: Jeremiah 31:10–14

Hear the word of God, O nations,
proclaim it on distant coasts and say:—

God who scattered Israel, now
gathers them together,
and guards them as shepherds
guard their flocks.

God will ransom the chosen
people
and redeem them from the hands
of their conquerors.

Shouting, they shall mount the
heights of Zion,
they shall come streaming to God's
blessings:
the grain, the wine, and the oil,
the sheep and the oxen;
they themselves shall be like
watered gardens,
never again shall they languish.

Then the young shall make merry
and dance,
old men and women as well.
I will turn their mourning into joy,
I will console and gladden them
after their sorrows.
I will lavish choice portions upon
them,
and my people shall be filled with
my blessings,
says our God. **Glory*....**

**Ant. 3 Let us build the city of
God!**

Psalm 48

O God, you are great and worthy
to be praised
in your holy city.
Your holy mountain rising in
beauty,
is the joy of all the earth.

Mount Zion, in the far north,
your holy city!
Within its citadels,
you show yourself its stronghold.

For invaders assembled together,
together they advanced.
As soon as they saw it, they were
astounded;
in panic they took to flight.

Trembling took hold of them there,
like the anguish of a woman giving
birth;
By the east wind you have
shattered the ships of Tarshish.

As we have heard, so we have seen
in the city of our God,
in the city of the Most High
which God establishes forever.

O God, we ponder your love
in the midst of your temple.
Your praise, like your name,
reaches to the ends of the earth.

With justice your hands are filled.
Let Mount Zion be glad!
The people of Judah rejoice
because of your judgments.

Walk through Zion, walk all round
it;
number its towers.
Review its ramparts,
examine its citadels;

that you may tell the next
generation
that this is our God,
our God forever and ever.
You will always be our guide.
        Glory*...

READING

RESPONSORY

I have seen the glory of God, in the land of the living. —**I have...**
You are with us always; —**in the...**
Glory to you, Source of all Being, Eternal Word and Holy Spirit.
   —**I have...**

CANTICLE OF ZECHARIAH

Ant. In love let us ponder your word forever.

INTERCESSIONS

O God, the path to holiness includes times of emptiness and
darkness;
      —let us realize that you are with us as you walked with
         Jesus on his journey toward the cross.
Holy, holy, holy are you, O God; the whole earth is full of your
glory;
      —help us to live compatibly with our environment.
The voice of God said, "Whom shall I send, and who will go for
us";
      —with your help, may I answer: "Here I am! Send me."
Jesus, you healed many who were sick with various diseases;
      —be with all healers and health care personnel as they give
         of themselves to care for us.
Jesus, you have called us to preach the good news by the
statement of our lives;
      —help us to live the truth with compassion.

PRAYER: Most gracious God and Father, you are with us as we
            make our journey throughout this day. Help us to
            look lovingly upon all people and events that come
            into our lives today and to walk gently upon our land.
            Grant this through Jesus who lives and walks among
            us ever present at each moment. Amen.

DAYTIME PRAYER

Ant. 1 I am a sojourner on earth; teach me your ways.
Psalm 119:17-24

Bless your servant that I may live
and obey your word.
Open my eyes that I may behold
the wonders of your law.

I am a sojourner on earth;
hide not your commands from me!
My soul is consumed with longing
forever, for your decrees.

You rebuke the insolent,
who turn from your commands.
Relieve me of their scorn and
   contempt,
for I have kept your word.

Though others sit plotting against
   me,
I ponder on your statutes.
Your will is my delight;
your decrees are my counselors.
   Glory*...

Ant. 2 Lead me in your truth, and guide me in the path of salvation.
Psalm 25

To you, O God, I lift up my soul.
In you, I trust, let me not be put to
   shame;
let not the wicked exult over me.
Those who wait on you shall not
   be put to shame;
but only those who wantonly
   break faith.

Make me know your ways, O God;
Teach me your paths.
Lead me in your truth, and teach
   me,—

for you are God, my savior.
For you I wait all the day long.

Remember your mercy, O God,
and your steadfast love,
which you have given from of old.
Remember not the sins of my
   youth, or my transgressions;
But in your goodness, remember
   me
according to your steadfast love!

You, O God, are good and upright.
You instruct sinners in your way.
You lead the humble in the right
   path;
you teach your way to the poor.

All your ways are loving and
   constant
for those who keep your covenant
   and your decrees.
For your name's sake, O God,
pardon my guilt, for it is great.
   Glory*...

Ant. 3 Say but the word, and I shall be healed.
II

Those who fear you, O God,
you will instruct in the way they
   should choose.
They shall abide in prosperity,
and their children shall possess
   the land.
Your friendship is for those who
   revere you;
make known to them your
   covenant.

My eyes are ever turned toward
   you,
for you rescue my feet from the
   snare.—

Turn to me and be gracious to me;
for I am lonely and afflicted.

Relieve the troubles of my heart
and bring me out of my distress.
See my affliction and my troubles,
and forgive all my sins.

See how many are my faults,
with what violence they pursue
me.—

Preserve my life and deliver me;
let me not be put to shame,
for I take refuge in you.
May integrity and uprightness
preserve me:
for my hope is in you.

Redeem Israel, O God, from all its
troubles. **Glory*...**

PRAYER: To you, O God, we lift up our hearts at this midday
prayer. We ask you to remember us and all those who
are troubled at this time. Help us to reach out in
justice and charity to those in need among us. Grant
this through the intercessions of all who served you in
serving your poor. Amen.

EVENING PRAYER

**Ant. 1 You heal my affliction;
you restore my soul to life!
Psalm 30**

I will praise you, O God, you have
rescued me
and have not let evil triumph over
me.

O God, I cried to you for help
and you have healed me.
You have raised my soul from the
dead,
restored me to life from among
those gone down to the grave.

We sing praises to you, we your
people,
and give thanks to your holy
name.
For your anger lasts but a
moment,
your favors for a lifetime.
At night there may be weeping,
but joy comes with the morning.

I said to myself in my prosperity,—

"Nothing will ever disturb me."
By your favor, O God,
you have made me strong as a
mountain;
when you hide your face, I am
dismayed.

O God, to you I cried,
to you I make supplication:
"What profit is there in my death,
if I go down to the grave?
Can dust praise you, or tell of your
faithfulness?"

Hear, O God, and be gracious to
me!
O God be my help!
You have turned my mourning
into dancing;
you have removed my sackcloth
and clothed me with gladness,
that I may praise you with full
voice,
and give thanks to you forever.
Glory*...

Ant. 2 In the integrity of my heart, I lay my guilt before you.
Psalm 32

Happy are they whose faults are
forgiven,
whose sins are covered.
Happy are they to whom our God
imputes no guilt,
in whose spirits there is no deceit.

When I declared not my sin,
my body wasted away
with groanings all the day long.
For day and night your hand was
heavy upon me;
my strength was dried up as by
the heat of summer.

When I acknowledged my sin to
you,
and did not hide my guilt;
I said: "I will confess my sins to
you, O God."
Then you did forgive me the guilt
of my sin.

So let all who acclaim you offer
prayers;
in times of distress, the rush of
the flood waters will not reach
them.
For you are a hiding place for me,
you preserve me from trouble;
you surround me with deliverance.

I will instruct you and teach you
the way you should go;
I will counsel you with my eye
upon you.
Be not like a horse or a mule,
without understanding,
which must be curbed with bit and
bridle else it will not keep you.

Many are the sorrows of the
wicked;—

but faithful love surrounds those
who trust in you.
We rejoice in you and are glad.
Let all the upright in heart rejoice
and shout for joy.
   Glory*...

Ant. 3 Behold the Lamb of God, who takes away the sins of the world.
Cant: Rev 11: 17–18; 12:10b–12a

We praise you, God Almighty,
who is and who was.
You have assumed your great
power,
you have begun your reign.

The nations have raged in anger,
but then came your day of wrath
and the moment to judge the
dead;
the time to reward your servants
the prophets
and the holy ones who revere you,
the great and the small alike.

Now have salvation and power
come,
your reign, O God, and the
authority of your Anointed One.
For the accusers of our loved ones
have been cast out,
who night and day accused them.

By the blood of the Lamb have
they been defeated,
and by the testimony of your
servants;
love for life did not deter them
from death.
So rejoice, you heavens,
and you that dwell therein!
   Glory*...

READING

RESPONSORY

You gather us together in the bosom of your love. —**You...**
As a mother hen, —**in the...**
Glory to you, Source of all Being, Eternal Word and

Holy Spirit. —**You...**

CANTICLE OF MARY

Ant. In you I rejoice all the days of my life.

INTERCESSIONS

Jesus, in the days of your ministry, many traveled far to listen to you;
  —keep alive our search for truth and our efforts to live by it.
You tell us not to be afraid;
  —let your Spirit guide the oppressed as they seek ways to freedom.
You call us "salt of the earth";
  —make us your true followers, one with the suffering of the world, and calling down God's blessing on your people.
You withdrew to lonely places, praying in the night;
  —remind us that you are with us in light or darkness, joy or sorrow; the abiding guest of our hearts.
Spirit of God, source of our deepest desires for good;
  —show us ways to be light for the world.

PRAYER: You, Mother and God, are our safety in times of distress. Show us your ways of peace that we may gather one another into your loving embrace, into your dwelling place. May you be with us this night and may all those in darkness walk in your light. Grant this, Spirit of Comfort, through Jesus, our brother. Amen.

FRIDAY

MORNING PRAYER

Ant 1 Create in me a clean heart, O God.

Psalm 51

Have mercy on me, O God, according to your steadfast love;—
in your abundant mercy blot out my sins.
Wash me thoroughly from my offenses,
and cleanse me from my sin!

For I know my offenses,
and my sin is ever before me.
Against you, you alone, have I
  sinned,
and done what is evil in your
  sight,
so you are justified in your
  sentence
and blameless in your judgment.
Behold, I was brought forth in a
  sinful world.

For you desire truth in my
  innermost being;
teach me wisdom in the depths of
  my heart.
O purify me, and I shall be clean;
O wash me, I shall be whiter than
  snow.
Fill me with joy and gladness;
let the bones you have broken
  rejoice.
Hide your face from my guilt,
and blot out all my offenses.

Create in me a clean heart,
put a steadfast spirit within me.
Cast me not from your presence,
take not your spirit from me.
Give me again the joy of your
  salvation,
with a willing spirit uphold me.

Then I will teach transgressors
  your ways,
and sinners will return to you.
Deliver me from death,
O God of my salvation,
and my tongue will sing out your
  saving help.

Open my lips, and my mouth will
  sing your praises.
For you take no delight in
  sacrifice;
were I to give a burnt offering,
you would not be pleased.
A broken spirit you accept;—

a contrite heart, you will not
  despise.

In your goodness, show favor to
  Zion;
rebuild the walls of Jerusalem.
Then you will delight in just
  sacrifices,
in gifts offered on your altar.
  Glory*...

**Ant. 2 You are our God, there is
no other besides you.**

Cant: Isaiah 45:15–25

Truly you are a God who is
  hidden,
the God of Israel, the savior!
They are put to shame and
  disgraced,
the makers of idols are put to
  confusion.

Israel, you are saved by the Most
  High
with everlasting salvation!
You shall never be put to shame
  or disgraced for all eternity.

For thus says the Most High,
the creator of the heavens,
who is God,
the designer and maker of the
  earth,
who established it,
not creating it as chaos,
but designing it to be lived in.

I am God, and there is no other.
I have not spoken in secret,
in a land of darkness;
I have not said to the
  descendants of my people,
"Look for me in chaos."
I, your God, speak the truth,
I declare what is right.

Come and assemble, gather
together,
you survivors of the nations!
They are without knowledge who
bear wooden idols
and pray to gods that cannot
save.

Come here and declare in counsel
together!
Who declared this from the
beginning
and foretold it from of old?
Was it not I, your God?
There is no other besides me,
a just and saving God!

Turn to me and be saved,
all you ends of the earth,
for I am God; there is no other!
By myself I have sworn,
uttering my just decree
and my word which cannot be
changed.

To me every knee shall bend;
by me every tongue shall swear,
saying, "Only in you, our God, are
justice and righteousness.

You, O God, shall be the
vindication and the glory
of all the descendants of Israel."
Glory*...

**Ant. 3 We are your people, the
sheep of your pasture.**

Psalm 100

All the earth cries out to you with
shouts of joy, O God,
Serving you with gladness;
coming before you, singing for
joy.

You, Creator of all, are God.
You made us, we belong to you,
we are your people, the sheep of
your pasture.

We enter your gates with
thanksgiving,
and your courts with songs of
praise!
We give you thanks and bless
your name.

Indeed, how good you are,
enduring, your steadfast love.
You are faithful to all generations.
Glory*...

READING

RESPONSORY

You are the Good Shepherd, have compassion on us. —**You are...**
In you we find mercy; —**have...**
Glory to you, Source of all Being, Eternal Word and Holy Spirit.
　—**You are...**

CANTICLE OF ZECHARIAH

Ant. You teach us the way of peace.

INTERCESSIONS

O God, you are Truth itself;
>—give us discerning hearts that we may live full and creative
> lives.

Jesus, you walked among the outcasts of your day, healing them
and drawing them to yourself;
>—help us to walk in your ways, that those who are shunned
> by society may know your love and healing through us.

Jesus, you bless with a hundredfold our endeavors to serve you;
>—give us the generosity to enable and support one another.

Spirit of God, you pray within us for needs we hardly know;
>—make our prayer one with yours that we may be one with
> you.

Eternal Shepherd, every person and the future of us all is
precious to you;
>—bless those who are tempted to take negative or destructive
> paths this day.

PRAYER: Forgiving God, look not upon our sins but upon our
desire to serve you and one another. Dispel our
darkness, and help us to embrace our failings in
loving union with your goodness. Heal us this day,
and may we be a source of strength and courage for
others. Grant this through the intercession of all
those who fill up what is wanting in the sufferings of
Christ. Amen.

DAYTIME PRAYER

Ant. 1 I cling to your will, O God.
   Psalm 119:25–32

My soul cleaves to the dust;
revive me according to your word!
I told of my ways, and you
   answered me;
teach me your statutes.

Make me understand the way of
   your precepts,
and I will ponder on your wonders.
My soul pines with sorrow;—

strengthen me by your word.

Keep me from the way of
   falsehood;
and teach me your law!
I have chosen the way of
   faithfulness,
I set your decrees before me.

I cling to your will, O God;
let me not be put to shame!
I will run in the way of your
   commands;—

when you enlighten my
understanding. **Glory*...**

**Ant. 2 I trust in God without
wavering.**

Psalm 26

Judge me, O God, for I walk in the
way of integrity,
I trust in you without wavering.

Examine me, O God, and try me;
test my heart and my mind,
for your steadfast love is before
me,
and I walk to you in faithfulness.

I do not sit with the wicked,
nor conspire with those who cause
trouble;
I avoid the company of evildoers;
and those who speak falsehood.

I wash my hands in innocence,
and gather around your altar,
singing a song of thanksgiving,
and telling of all your wonders.

I love the house where you live,
the place where your glory dwells.
Do not sweep me away with
sinners,
nor my life with those who
oppress,
who plot evil deeds,
whose hands are full of bribes.

As for me, I walk the path of
integrity.
Redeem me, and be gracious to
me.—

My foot stands on level ground;
I will bless you in the assembly.
Glory*...

**Ant. 3 I call to you, O God, hear
the sound of my voice.**

Psalm 28:1–3, 6–9

To you, O God, I call,
my rock, be not deaf to me.
If you turn your ear away from me,
I become like those in the grave.

Hear the voice of my pleading
as I cry to you for help,
as I lift up my hands in prayer
to your holy sanctuary.

Do not take me away with the
wicked,
with those who are workers of evil,
who speak peace with their
neighbors,
while evil is in their hearts.

I bless you, for you have heard
the voice of my supplication.
You are my strength and my
shield;
in you my heart trusts.
I am helped, and my heart exults,
with my song I give you thanks.

You are the strength of your
people,
you are the refuge of your
anointed.
Save your people; and bless your
heritage;
be their shepherd and carry them
forever. **Glory*...**

PRAYER: Jesus, our Redeemer, you brought us into life by dying
upon the cross. May we search for new ways to
alleviate suffering among all creatures that your name
be glorified and that peace may find a home in us. We

ask this in the name of all creation that **groans** for your salvation to be realized within its being. Amen.

EVENING PRAYER

Ant. 1 Be gracious to me, O God, for I have sinned.

Psalm 41

Blessed are they who consider the poor!
O God, you deliver them in the day of trouble;
you guard them and give them life;
they are called blessed in the land;
you do not give them up to temptation.
You sustain them on their sickbeds;
you heal them of all their infirmities.

As for me, I said: "O God, be gracious to me,
heal me, for I have sinned against you."
Some could say of me in malice:
"When will you die and your name perish?"
They come to see me, uttering empty words,
while their hearts gather mischief;
and spread it abroad.
They whisper about me,
imagining the worst of me.

They say, "A deadly thing has come upon you;
you will not rise from where you lie."
Even my friend in whom I trusted,—

who ate of my bread, has turned against me.

But you, O God, be gracious to me.
Raise me up in your great mercy.
By this I shall know that you are pleased with me,
that evildoers have not triumphed.
You have upheld me in my integrity,
and set me in your presence forever.

Blessed are you, God of Israel,
from everlasting to everlasting.
Amen. Amen. **Glory*...**

Ant. 2 In the stillness we will hear your voice.

Psalm 46

God is our refuge and strength,
a helper in time of trouble.
We shall not fear though the earth should rock,
though the mountains fall into the depths of the sea,
though its waters rage and foam,
though the mountains tremble with its tumult.

There is a river whose streams gladden the city of God,
the holy place of the Most High.
God is within, it shall not be moved;—

God will help it at the dawning
of the day.
Nations rage, sovereignties are
shaken;
at the sound of God's voice, the
earth melts away.

The God of hosts is with us;
the God of our ancestors is our
refuge.

Come, behold the works of our
God,
who has wrought wonders on
the earth.
Making wars cease to the ends
of the earth;
breaking the bow, snapping the
spear,
burning the chariots with fire.
"Be still, and know that I am
God,
I am exalted among the nations,
I am exalted on the earth!"

The God of hosts is with us;
the God of our ancestors is our
refuge. **Glory*....**

**Ant. 3 You are the ruler of all
the ages, O God.**
Cant: Rev 15:3-4

Great and wonderful are your
works,
God the Almighty One!
Just and true are your ways,
Ruler of all the ages!

Who shall refuse you honor,
or the glory due your name?

For you alone are holy,
all nations shall come and
worship in your presence.
Your judgments are clearly
seen.
Glory*...

READING

RESPONSORY

In the spirit of Jesus, we give praise to our God. —**In the...**
For our sins are forgiven; —**we give...**
Glory to you, Source of all Being, Eternal Word and Holy Spirit.
—**In the...**

CANTICLE OF MARY

Ant. Your covenant is one of mercy and forgiveness.

INTERCESSIONS

The law of God is perfect, refreshing the soul;
—let your love, O God, be our law of life and perfect guide.
Your forgiveness of humankind flows from generation to
generation;
—heal the nations that continue to seek vengeance; teach us
all how to forgive in the name of Jesus.

Jesus, you stayed in desert places, strengthened there by God.
  —In time of pain or trouble, help us to find God in the solitude
    of our hearts.
You are our hope in life and in death;
  —help us to live our belief in you for the strength and courage
    of all in need of your truth.
Spirit of God, your gifts abound in humankind;
  —bless the poor whose creativity is buried by a raw search
    for survival.

PRAYER: Jesus, you heal the sick and brokenhearted. Let your
    mercy be upon us so that we may be a sign of your
    mercy in our world. We thank you for your forgiveness
    and for bringing us to this time of our lives. May all
    those who died find rest in you. Grant this through the
    intercession of all who died forgiving those who
    oppressed them. Amen.

SATURDAY

MORNING PRAYER

**Ant. 1 Before the dawn, O God,
hear my call for help.
Psalm 119: 145–152**

With all my heart, I cry to you;
answer me, O God.
I cry to you; save me,
that I may observe your will.

I rise before dawn and cry for help;
I hope in your words.
My eyes watch throughout the
  night
meditating on your promises.

Hear my voice in your steadfast
  love;
in your justice preserve my life.
Those who persecute me draw
  near;
they are far from your law.

But you, O God, are near at hand,
all your commands are true.—

Long have I known that your will
  endures forever.   **Glory*...**

**Ant. 2 Bring me to your holy
mountain, the place of your
dwelling.
Cant: Exodus 15:1–4a, 8–13,
17–18**

I will sing to you, O God, for you
  are gloriously triumphant;
horse and rider you have cast into
  the sea.

You are my strength and my
  courage,
you are my salvation.
You are my God, I praise you;
God of my ancestors, I extol you.

Pharaoh's chariots and army you
  cast into the sea.
At a breath of your anger the
  waters piled up,—

the floods stood up in a heap;
the floods congealed in the midst
of the sea.

The enemy boasted, "I will pursue
and overtake them;
I will divide the spoils and have
my fill of them;
I will draw my sword; my hand
shall destroy them!"
When your wind blew, the sea
covered them;
they sank as lead in the mighty
waters.

Who is like you, among the gods?
Who is like you, majestic in
holiness,
terrible in glorious deeds, worker
of wonders?
You stretched out your hand, the
earth swallowed them!

In your love you led the people
you redeemed;
you guided them to your holy
dwelling.

You bring them in and plant them
on your mountain,
the place you have made for your
abode,
the sanctuary which your hands
have established.
You, O God, will reign forever and
ever. **Glory*...**

**Ant. 3 O praise God all you
nations.**

Psalm 117

Praise our God, all you nations!
Acclaim the Most High, all you
peoples!

For great is your love for us;
and your faithfulness endures
forever. **Glory*...**

READING

RESPONSORY

Your love is round about me; in you I find my life. —**Your love...**
Forever I will sing your praise; —**in you...**
Glory to you, Source of all Being, Eternal Word and Holy Spirit.
     —**Your love...**

CANTICLE OF ZECHARIAH

Ant. You are the light of my salvation.

INTERCESSIONS

O God, your son Jesus prayed that we all may be one;
     —help us to love one another as you love us.
All of creation cries out for healing;
     —make us instruments of your peace.
You are the Center of all that is;
     —teach us to listen to your life within us.
Many do not know your love and care for us;
     —let our lives bear witness to your unending mercy.

You call us to live in freedom and happiness;
—give hope and peace of heart to all in prison or bondage
of any kind.

PRAYER: You give and sustain our lives, O God, and in you we
find our sanctuary. May all displaced people find a
place of sanctuary and safety in our hearts and
homes this day, and may all those who seek you find
you in the living word among us. Grant this through
Jesus who lives and reigns among us. Amen.

DAYTIME PRAYER

Ant. 1 Incline my heart to your decrees.
Psalm 119:33–40

Teach me the way of your
  precepts,
and I will keep them to the end.
Give me understanding,
that I may keep your law
and observe it with all my heart.

Guide me in the path of your
  commandments,
for there is my delight.
Incline my heart to your will
and not to love of profit.

Turn my eyes from what is vain;
by your ways, give me life.
Keep the promise you have made
to those who reverence you.

Turn away the reproach which I
  dread;
for your decrees are good.
Behold, I long for your precepts;
in your justice, give me life!
  Glory*...

Ant. 2 O taste and see the goodness of our God!
Psalm 34

I will bless you, O God, at all
  times,
your praise always on my lips.
My soul makes its boast in you;
the afflicted shall hear and be
  glad.
Glorify our God with me.
Together let us praise God's
  name.

I sought you, and you answered
  me;
and delivered me from all my
  fears.
Look towards the Most High, and
  be radiant;
let your faces not be ashamed.
These poor ones cried; you heard
  them,
and saved them from all their
  troubles.

Your angel, O God, is encamped
around those who revere you, to
deliver them.
Taste and see that God is good!
Happy are they who take refuge
in you.

May all the saints revere you, O
God.
Those who revere you, have no
want!
Young lions suffer want and
hunger;
but those who seek you lack no
blessing. **Glory*...**

**Ant. 3 Blessed are those who
seek after peace.**
II

Come, children, listen to me,
I will teach you to reverence the
Most High.
Who among you longs for life
and many days to enjoy
prosperity?

Keep your tongue from evil,
your lips from speaking deceit.
Turn aside from evil and do good;
seek peace and pursue it.

God's eyes are turned to the
righteous,
God's ears toward their cry.
God's face turns away from evil,
that it not be remembered on
earth.

When the just cry, the Most High
hears,
and delivers them from their
troubles.
God is close to the
brokenhearted;
saving those whose spirits are
crushed.

Many are the afflictions of the
just;
they will be delivered from them
all.
God will keep guard over all their
bones,
not one of them shall be broken.

Evil shall be its own destruction;
oppression shall be condemned.
You redeem the lives of your
servants;
those who take refuge in you
shall not be condemned.
Glory*...

PRAYER: Most provident God, you graciously give us all good
gifts. Teach us to care for our earth: to till our soil
responsibly, to keep our air pure, to free our waters
from pollution, to harvest the warmth of our sun, and to
respect the rights of all species. May we willingly share
the gifts of your goodness with one another. We ask this
of you, God of our universe. Amen.

WEEK II

SUNDAY, EVENING PRAYER I

Ant. 1 Your word, O God, is a light for my path.

Psalm 119:105–112

O God, your word is a lamp to my feet
and a light for my path.
I have sworn an oath and confirmed it,
to observe your commandments.

I am sorely afflicted:
give me life according to your word!
Accept my offerings of praise,
and teach me your decrees.

Though I hold my life in my hands,
I do not forget your law.
Though the wicked try to ensnare me,
I do not stray from your precepts.

Your will is my heritage forever,
the joy of my heart.
I incline my heart to carry out your will forever, to endless ages. **Glory*...**

Ant. 2 I have given you as a covenant to the people.

Psalm 16

Preserve me, O God, for in you I take refuge.—

*Glory to you, Source of all Being, Eternal Word, and Holy Spirit.

As it was in the beginning is now and will be forever. Amen.

I say to you: "You are my God;
I have no good apart from you."
All my delight is in your saints;
the faithful who dwell in your land.

Those who choose other gods increase their sorrows;
their offerings of blood I will not pour out
or take their names upon my lips.

You are my portion and my cup;
you are my fortune, my prize.
The lines have fallen for me in pleasant places;
I have been given a welcome heritage.

I will bless you who give me counsel;
in the night my heart instructs me.
I keep you always before me;
because you are near, I shall stand firm.

Therefore my heart is glad, and my soul rejoices;
even my body rests securely.
For you do not give me up to death,
or let your faithful see the grave.

You will show me the path of life;
in your presence there is fullness of joy,
in your hands, happiness forever. **Glory*...**

Ant. 3 For me to live is Christ and to die is gain.

Cant: Phil 2:6–11

Though he was in the form of God,
Jesus did not count equality with God
something to be grasped at.

But emptied himself
taking the form of a slave,
being born in human likeness.

Being found in human estate,
he humbled himself and became obedient,—

obediently accepting death, even death on a cross!

Therefore God has highly exalted him
and bestowed on him the name above every other name.

So that at the name of Jesus
every knee should bow,
in heaven, on the earth,
and under the earth,
and every tongue proclaim
to the glory of God:
Jesus Christ is Lord! **Glory*...**

READING

RESPONSORY

We call to you in our need, O God, for you hear the cry of the poor.
—**We call...**
You will not leave us orphans; —**for you...**
Glory to you, Source of all Being, Eternal Word and Holy Spirit.
—**We call...**

CANTICLE OF MARY

Ant. Be mindful of your mercy to us, O loving God.

INTERCESSIONS

O God, you grieve for all that afflicts us;
—give those who struggle with addictions the courage and perseverance they need.
You are father and mother to us, and we bask in your love;
—inspire persons of integrity and compassion to care for children who are separated from their parents.
You bless those who employ the talents you have given them;
—give all in research the insight they need to develop the good you desire for us.
Jesus, you loved the land and fields of flowers;
—bless farmers and all who are stewards of the soil.

You taught your followers to travel lightly through life;
—call our consumer culture to a change of heart—to values
that lead to life.

PRAYER: O God, we long to love you with all our heart and mind
and soul, but we know we are divided. Give us a single
heart. Make us one as you are one with Jesus and your
Holy Spirit. Amen.

MORNING PRAYER

**Ant. 1 You are members of the
household of God.**

Psalm 118

We give thanks to you, for you are
good,
and your steadfast love endures
forever.

Let the descendants of Israel say:
"Your steadfast love endures
forever."
Let the descendants of Aaron say:
"Your steadfast love endures
forever."
Let those who fear you say:
"Your steadfast love endures
forever."

In my distress, I called to you;
you answered me and set me free.
With you at my side, I do not fear.
What can anyone do against me?
You are at my side to help me:
I shall withstand all evildoers.

It is better to take refuge in you,
than to trust in people:
it is better to take refuge in you
than to trust in our leaders.

All wickedness surrounded me;
in your name I crushed it.
It surrounded me like bees;—

it blazed like a fire among thorns.
In your name I crushed it.

I was pushed hard, and was falling
but you came to help me.
You are my strength and my song;
you are my salvation.

O God, you have triumphed;
your reign is exalted.
You have triumphed over all;
I shall not die, I shall live
and recount your wondrous deeds.
You have chastened me sorely,
but have not given me over to
death.

Open to me the gates of justice,
that I may enter and give thanks.
This is your gate, O God;
the just shall enter through it.
I thank you for you have answered
me
you alone are my salvation.

The stone which the builders
rejected
has become the cornerstone.
This is your doing, O God;
it is marvelous in our eyes.
This is the day which you have
made;
let us rejoice and be glad in it.

Save us, we beseech you, O God!
O God, grant us success.—

Blessed are those who enter in
your holy name.
For you O God, are our God,
and you have given us light.

Let us go forward in procession
with branches,
up to your holy altar.
You are my God, I thank you.
You are my God, I praise you.
We give thanks to you for you are
good;
and your steadfast love endures
forever. **Glory*...**

**Ant. 2 How glorious is your name
over all the earth.**
Cant: Daniel 3:52–57

Blessed are you, God of our
ancestors,
praiseworthy and exalted above all
forever.

Blessed be your holy and glorious
name,
praiseworthy and exalted above all
for all ages.

Blessed are you in the temple of
your glory,
praiseworthy and exalted above all
forever.

Blessed are you on the throne of
your kindom,
praiseworthy and exalted above all
forever.

Blessed are you who look into the
depths
from your throne upon the
cherubim,
praiseworthy and exalted above all
forever.

Blessed are you in the firmament of
heaven,
praiseworthy and glorious forever.

Blessed are you by all your works.
We praise and exalt you above all
forever. **Glory*...**

**Ant. 3 Let us praise God's infinite
greatness.**
Psalm 150

We praise you, O God, in your holy
sanctuary;
we praise you in your mighty
heavens.
We praise you for your powerful
deeds;
we praise you according to your
greatness.

We praise you with trumpet sound;
We praise you with lute and harp!
We praise you with strings and
pipe!

We praise you with sounding
cymbals,
We praise you with clashing
cymbals!
Let everything that breathes,
give praise to you, O God.
Glory*...

READING

RESPONSORY

Our hearts are restless, O God, till they rest in you. —**Our...**
Searching and waiting; —**till they...**
Glory to you, Source of all Being, Eternal Word and Holy Spirit.
—**Our...**

CANTICLE OF ZECHARIAH

Ant. May you give light to those who sit in darkness.

INTERCESSIONS

God revealing, forgiving, ever recreating us;
—we thank you for your abiding care, and we pray for those who
do not know your love.
You are a God of the living, and your Spirit brings us joy;
—let our lives bear witness to the resurrection of Jesus.
Minorities, countries, the earth itself—all cry out for liberation as
never before;
—Spirit of God, flood our lives with the wisdom to make all
things new.
You raise up prophets today;
—open our hearts, our church, and our world to their message.
Jesus, your message calls for the new wineskins of openness to
your word;
—help us to free ourselves from what is merely familiar and
comfortable.

PRAYER: O God, on this first day of the week, we join all
creation and people of all ages in praising you. Your
kindness and forgiveness flow like a river through the
centuries, refreshing our faith, our hope and our love.
May you be forever praised throughout all the ages.
Amen.

DAYTIME PRAYER

**Ant. 1 You restore my soul in
your living waters.**

Psalm 23

O God, you are my shepherd;
I shall not want.
You make me to lie in green
pastures.
You lead me to restful waters,
to restore my soul.

You guide me in paths of
righteousness—

for the sake of your name.
Even though I walk through the
valley of the shadow of death,
I fear no evil;
for you are with me;
your crook and your staff
give me comfort.

You prepare a table before me
in the presence of my foes;
you anoint my head with oil,
my cup overflows.

Surely goodness and mercy shall
  follow me
all the days of my life;
and I shall dwell in your holy
  house forever and ever. **Glory*...**

**Ant. 2 Lead a life worthy of God,
who calls you to glory.**
Psalm 76

In Judah you are made known, O
  God,
your name is great in Israel.
Your abode is established in
  Jerusalem,
your dwelling place in Zion.
There you broke the flashing
  arrows,
the shield, the sword, the weapons
  of war.

You, O God, are glorious,
more majestic than the mountains.
The stouthearted were stripped of
  their spoil;
they sank into sleep;
all the provokers of war—

were unable to use their hands.
At your rebuke, O God, our God,
both rider and horse lay stunned.
  Glory*...

**Ant. 3 Do not let the sun go down
on your anger, for God is a
forgiving God.**
II

You, you alone, strike terror.
When your anger is aroused,
who can stand before you?
From heaven you utter judgment;
the earth feared and stood still,
when you arose to give judgment
to save the oppressed of the earth.

Our anger will serve to praise you;
its residue gird you round.
We fulfill the vows made before
  you;
you whom we revere,
who cut short the lives of leaders,
who strike terror in unjust rulers.
  Glory*...

PRAYER: O God, you have created us to be free. Only through
the power of your love do you reign over us. Help us to
be worthy of the gift of freedom, and teach us to respect
all creation as the work of your hands. We ask this,
Creator God, giver of all good gifts, through Jesus who
taught us the way. Amen.

EVENING PRAYER II

**Ant. 1 You are a priestly people
according to the order of
Melchizedeck.**

Psalm 110:1-5, 7

God's revelation to the Anointed
  One:
"Sit at my side:—

till I put injustice beneath your
  feet."

God will send forth from Zion
your scepter of power:
rule in the midst of your foes.

Your people will give themselves
  freely—

on the day you lead your host
upon the holy mountains.
From the womb of the morning
your youth will come like dew.

God has sworn an oath that will
    not be changed.
"You are a priest forever,
after the order of Melchizedek."

The Anointed standing by your
    side,
will shatter rulers on the day of
    wrath.

Drinking from your streams by
    the wayside
shall the Chosen One be
    refreshed. **Glory*...**

**Ant. 2 The heavens belong to
you, but the earth has been
given to us.**
                Psalm 115

Not to us, O God, not to us,
but to your name give glory
for the sake of your love and your
    truth!
Why should the nations say,
"Where is their God?"

But you are in the heavens;
you do whatever you please.
Their idols are silver and gold,
the work of human hands.

They have mouths, but cannot
    speak;
eyes, but cannot see;
they have ears, but cannot hear;
noses, but cannot smell.

They have hands, but cannot feel;
feet, but cannot walk.
No sound comes from their
    throats.—

Those who make them are like
    them;
so are all who trust in them.

Descendants of Abraham, trust in
    God,
who is your help and your shield.
Descendants of Sarah, trust in
    God,
who is your help and your shield.
You who fear, trust in God,
who is your help and your shield.

You remember us and will bless
    us,
blessing the descendants of
    Abraham,
blessing the descendants of
    Sarah.
God will bless those who fear,
the little no less than the great.

May God give you increase,
you and all your children.
May you be blessed by the Most
    High,
who made heaven and earth!

The heavens belong to God,
but the earth has been given to
    us.
The dead do not praise you,
nor those who go down into
    silence.
But we who live, bless you,
both now and forever. Amen.
    Glory*...

**Ant. 3 We come to join in your
holy banquet, O God.**

        Cant: Rev 19:1, 5–7

Salvation, glory, and power
    belong to you,
your judgments are honest and
    true.

All of us, your servants, sing
  praise to you,
we worship you reverently, both
  great and small.
You, our almighty God, are
  Creator of heaven and earth.—

Let us rejoice and exult, and give
  you glory.

The wedding feast of the Lamb
  has begun,
And the bride has made herself
  ready. **Glory*...**

READING

RESPONSORY

How can we repay you, O God, for your goodness to us?
  —How can...
We will sing your praise; **—for your...**
Glory to you, Source of all Being, Eternal Word and Holy Spirit.
  —How can...

CANTICLE OF MARY

Ant. My spirit rejoices in God, my Savior.

INTERCESSIONS

Rain and clouds are your gifts of life and beauty to us, O God;
  —teach us how to use and preserve the waters of the earth.
You surround us with beauty on earth and in the sky;
  —bless those who have lost the gift of sight.
You are always with us, silently guiding and encouraging us;
  —help us to quiet our lives with moments for listening to your
    voice in our hearts.
You love justice, and all your ways are true;
  —give us the insight and courage to face our prejudices and
    blind spots.
Jesus is your supreme gift to us;
  —let the words of his gospel be woven into our daily lives,
    coming easily to mind for our inspiration and your glory.

PRAYER: God of mystery, God of love, send your Spirit into our
hearts with gifts of wisdom and peace, fortitude and
charity. We long to love and serve you. Faithful God,
make us faithful. This we ask through the intercession
of all your saints. Amen.

MONDAY

MORNING PRAYER

Ant 1 When from this exile shall we behold you face to face?

Psalm 42

Like the deer that yearns
for flowing streams,
so my soul is longing
for you, my God.

My soul is thirsting for God,
the living God.
When shall I come and see,
the face of God?

My tears have become my food,
by night and day,
while I hear it said all day,
"Where is your God?"

These things will I remember
as I pour out my soul:
how I led the throng,
to the house of God,
with shouts of gladness and
songs of thanksgiving,
the multitude keeping festival.

Why are you cast down my soul,
why disquieted within me?
Hope in God; I will again praise
you,
my help and my God.

My soul is cast down within me,
therefore I think of you
from the land of Jordan and of
Hermon,
from Mount Mizar.

Deep calls to deep,
in the thunder of your waters;
all your waves and your billows
have swept over me.

By day you will send me—

your steadfast love;
and at night your song is with
me,
a prayer to the God of my life.

I will say to you my rock:
"Why have you forgotten me?
Why do I go mourning
because of oppression?"

As with a deadly wound,
my adversaries taunt me,
saying to me all the day long:
"Where is your God?"

Why are you cast down, my soul,
why disquieted within me?
Hope in God; for I shall praise
again,
my savior and my God.
    Glory*...

Ant. 2 Worker of wonders, show forth your splendor!
    Cant: Sirach 36:1-5, 10-13

Come to our aid, O God of the
universe,
and put all the nations in dread
of you!
Raise your hand toward the
heathen,
that they may realize your power.

As you have used us to show
them your holiness,
so now use them to show us your
glory.
Thus they will know, as we know,
that there is no God but you.

Give new signs and work new
wonders;
show forth the splendor of the
works of your hands.

Gather all the tribes of Jacob,
that they may inherit the land as
of old.
Show mercy to the people called
by your name;
Israel, whom you named your
first-born.

Take pity on your holy city,
Jerusalem, your dwelling place.
Fill Zion with your majesty,
your temple with your glory.
Glory*...

**Ant. 3 The courts of heaven
ring with the praise of our
God.**

Psalm 19a

The heavens tell of your glory, O
God,
and the firmament proclaims your
handiwork.—

Day unto day pours forth the
story
and night unto night reveals its
knowledge.

No speech, no word, no voice is
heard;
yet their voice goes out to all the
earth,
their words to the end of the
world.

In them you set a tent for the
sun;
it comes forth like a bridegroom
leaving his chamber,
rejoices like a champion running
its course.

Its rising is from the end of the
heavens,
and its course to the end of them;
there is nothing concealed from
its heat. **Glory*...**

READING

RESPONSORY

You are present to us, O God, in all creation. **—You are...**
Enriching our lives; **—in all...**
Glory to you, Source of all Being, Eternal Word and Holy Spirit.
—You are...

CANTICLE OF ZECHARIAH

Ant. Blessed be God who has visited us and saved us.

INTERCESSIONS

O God, you ask us to keep your words in our minds and hearts
and so we pray:
   —give us the grace to hear you in turmoil and in silence.
Help us to recognize our sinfulness and to be grateful for your
gifts of grace;
   —give us the strength and courage to act in humility and truth.

God of wisdom and source of all that is sacred;
—help teachers to value and nourish the wisdom and goodness
of children.
Jesus, you came to serve and not to be served;
—bless all who serve us daily, in inclement weather, in
dangerous jobs, and at work that is tedious or monotonous.
We are blessed by the words of your gospel;
—make us aware of the ways we shield ourselves from its
challenge to us.

PRAYER: O God, you have made us in your image and we long to
see your face. Quiet our minds and enkindle our
hearts, that walking the way of your truth we may leave
the imprint of your goodness throughout the world.
Grant this in the name of Jesus. Amen.

DAYTIME PRAYER

**Ant. 1 Make love your aim, and
desire every spiritual gift.**

Psalm 119:41–48

O God, let your love come upon
me,
your salvation according to your
promise;
Then I have answer for those who
taunt me,
for I trust in your word.

Take not truth from my mouth,
for my hope is in your decrees.
I shall always keep your law
forever and ever.

I shall walk in the path of
freedom,
for I have sought your precepts.
I will speak of your will before
rulers
and shall not be put to shame;

for my delight is in your
commandments;
these I have loved.—

I revere your precepts,
and will ponder on your statutes.
Glory*...

**Ant. 2 My delight is to do your
will, O God.**

Psalm 40:2–14, 17–18

I waited patiently for you, O God
and you stooped down to me;
and heard my cry.

You drew me from the desolate
pit,
out of the miry clay,
and set my feet upon a rock,
making my steps secure.

You put a new song in my mouth,
a song of praise to you.
Many shall see and fear
and place their trust in you.

Happy are we who have placed
our trust in you, O God,
who do not turn to the proud,
to those who follow false gods!

For us you have multiplied, O
  God, my Creator,
your wondrous deeds and plans;
none can compare with you!
Were I to proclaim and tell of
  them,
they are more than can be
  numbered.

Sacrifice and offering you do not
  desire;
but you have given me an open
  ear.
Burnt offering and sin offering
  you have not required.

Therefore, I said, "Here I am;
In the scroll of the book it is
  written of me:
my delight is to do your will;
your law is within my heart."
  Glory*...

**Ant. 3 Your mercy is from age
to age toward those who
revere you.**
  II

Your deliverance I have
  proclaimed
in the great assembly.
I have not restrained my lips,
as you well know, O God.

I have not concealed your saving
  help within my heart;
but have spoken of your
  faithfulness, and your salvation;
I have not hidden your steadfast
  love nor your faithfulness
from the great assembly.

O God, you will not withhold
your mercy from me.
Your steadfast love and
  faithfulness always surround
  me.

For evils without number have
  encompassed me;
My sins have overtaken me,
till I cannot see.
They are more than the hairs of
  my head;
my heart fails me.

Be pleased, O God, to deliver me!
O God, make haste to help me!

May all who seek you rejoice and
  be glad;
May all who love your salvation
say evermore: "Great is our God!"

As for me, I am poor and needy;
but you take thought of me.
You are my help, my deliverer;
O God, do not delay.
  Glory*...

PRAYER: God of justice, God of mercy, bless all those who are
surprised with pain this day from suffering caused by
their own weakness or that of others. Let what we
suffer teach us to be merciful; let our sins teach us to
forgive. This we ask through the intercession of Jesus
and all who died forgiving those who oppressed them.
Amen.

EVENING PRAYER

Ant. 1 O God, how great is your wisdom, so far beyond my understanding.

Psalm 139:1–18, 23–24

O God, you have searched me
and you know me,
you know when I sit and when I
stand;
you discern my thoughts from
afar.
You mark when I walk or lie
down,
with all my ways you are
acquainted.

Before a word is on my tongue,
behold, O God, you know the
whole of it.
Behind and before you besiege
me,
You lay your hand upon me.
Such knowledge is too wonderful
for me:
too high, beyond my reach.

O where can I go from your spirit,
or where can I flee from your
presence?
If I climb to heaven, you are
there!
If I lie in the grave, you are there!

If I take the wings of the morning
and dwell in the depths of the
sea,
even there your hand shall lead
me,
your hand shall hold me fast.

If I say: "Let darkness cover me,
and the light around me be
night,"
even darkness is not dark to
you,—

and the night is as bright as the
day;
for darkness is as light to you.
Glory*...

Ant. 2 You search the mind and probe the heart, giving to each as we deserve.

II

For it was you who formed my
inmost parts,
knit me together in my mother's
womb.
I praise you for the wonder of my
being,
for the wonder of all your works.

Already you knew me well;
my body was not hidden from
you,
when I was being made in secret
and molded in the depths of the
earth.

Your eyes beheld my unformed
substance;
in your book they all were
written,
the days that you had formed for
me,
when none of them yet were.

How precious to me are your
thoughts!
How vast the sum of them!
If I count them, they are more
than the sand.
When I awake, I am still with you.

Search me, O God, and know my
heart!
O test me and know my thoughts!
See that I follow not the wrong
way,—

and lead me in the way of life
eternal. **Glory*...**

**Ant. 3 May Christ dwell in our
hearts through faith that we
may be rooted in love.**
Cant: Ephesians 1:3–10

Praised be the God
of our Lord Jesus Christ,
who has blessed us in Christ
with every spiritual blessing in
the heavens.

God chose us in him
before the foundation of the
world,
that we should be holy
and blameless in God's sight.

We have been predestined
to be God's children through
Jesus Christ,—

such was the purpose of God's
will,
that all might praise the glorious
favor
bestowed on us in Christ.

In Christ and through his blood,
we have redemption,
the forgiveness of our sins,
according to the riches of God's
grace lavished upon us.

For God has made known to us
in all wisdom and insight,
the mystery of the plan set forth
in Christ.

A plan to be carried out in Christ,
in the fullness of time,
to unite all things in Christ,
things in heaven and things on
earth. **Glory*...**

READING

RESPONSORY

You create us in your image, O God, we are co-creators with you.
   —You create...
We are nothing without you; **—we are...**
Glory to you, Source of all Being, Eternal Word and Holy Spirit.
   —You create...

CANTICLE OF MARY

Ant. I rejoice in your greatness, O God.

INTERCESSIONS

O God, you invite us to: "Let light shine out of darkness";
   —give us the courage to embrace the darkness and walk with
   you toward the light.
You hear the prayers of those in need;
   —give us the grace to open our hearts, our homes, and our
   spaces of worship to those who are in distress.

You marveled at the faith of the Centurion;
  —help us to recognize that truth and wisdom are often found
  where we least expect.
Spirit of God, guide us in our use of power;
  —let our methods be constructive and sensitive to the needs
  of all.
May we realize that life itself is a blessing;
  —comfort those who are preparing for the blessings of
  eternal life.

PRAYER: God of wisdom, God of our way, we have walked with
you from early morning. Renew our strength this night
that we may rise to serve you and one another with
clear vision and strong hope. We pray especially for all
who will awake this night to the vision of your glory.
This we ask through Jesus who is the light of the
world. Amen.

TUESDAY

MORNING PRAYER

**Ant. 1 O God, let us walk as
people of light, that we may
know what is pleasing to you.**

Psalm 43

Defend me, O God, and plead my
  cause against a godless nation.
From the deceitful and the unjust
rescue me, O God.

For in you I take refuge;
why have you cast me off?
Why do I go mourning
because of oppression?

O send out your light and your
  truth;
let these be my guide.
Let them bring me to your holy hill
and to your dwelling place.

Then I will go to the altar of God,
to God, my exceeding joy;
and I will praise you with the lyre,
O God, my God.

Why are you cast down, my soul,
why groan within me?
Hope in God;
I shall again praise, my savior and
  my God. **Glory*...**

**Ant. 2 Seek first the reign of God,
and all things shall be yours as
well.**

      **Cant: Isaiah 38:10–14,
        17b–20**

Once I said,
"In the noontime of life, I must
  depart!
I am consigned to the gates of
  death for the rest of my years."

I said, "I shall not see God
in the land of the living.
No longer shall I see my
    companions
among the dwellers of this world."

My dwelling is plucked up and
    removed from me
like a shepherd's tent;
like a weaver I have rolled up my
    life;
being cut off from the loom.

Day and night you give me over to
    torment;
I cry for help until daybreak;
like a lion you break all my bones;
day and night you give me over to
    torment.

Like a swallow or crane, I clamor,
I moan like a dove.
My eyes grow weary gazing upward.
I am oppressed; be my security!

Restore me to health, make me live!
It was for my welfare that I had
    great bitterness;
you have held back my life from the
    pit of destruction,
you have cast all my sins behind
    your back.

For the nether world cannot thank
    you,
death cannot praise you;
those who go down to the pit
cannot hope for your faithfulness.

The living, the living give you
    thanks, as I do this day;
Parents make known to their
    children,
O God, your faithfulness.

You, O God, will save us;
we will sing to stringed
    instruments—

all the days of our lives,
in your holy dwelling.
    Glory*...

**Ant. 3 Consider the lilies of the
field; they neither toil nor spin.
Psalm 65**

Praise is due to you,
O God in Zion;
and to you shall vows be made,
to you who hear our prayer.

To you shall all flesh come because
    of its sins.
When our offenses bear us down,
you forgive them all.

Blessed are we whom you choose
    and draw near,
to dwell in your courts!
We are filled with the goodness of
    your house,
your holy temple!

With wonders you deliver us,
O God of our salvation.
You are the hope of all the earth
and of far distant seas.

By your strength, you established
    the mountains,
girded with might;
you still the roaring of the seas,
the roaring of their waves,
and the tumult of the peoples.

Those who dwell at earth's farthest
    bounds
stand in awe at your wonders;
you make the sunrise and sunset
    shout for joy.

You care for the earth, give it water,
you fill it with riches.
Your river in heaven brims over
to provide its grain.

You visit the earth and water it,
greatly enriching it;
you level it, soften it with showers,
blessing its growth.

You crown the year with your
bounty;
Abundance flows in your path.
The pastures of the wilderness
flow,—

the hills gird themselves with joy,
the meadows clothe themselves
with flocks,
the valleys deck themselves with
grain,
they shout and sing together for
joy. **Glory*...**

READING

RESPONSORY

You know our frailty, O God; give us strength. —**You know...**
You fill us with hope; —**give...**
Glory to you, Source of all Being, Eternal Word and Holy Spirit.
  —**You know...**

CANTICLE OF ZECHARIAH

Ant. You, O God, have raised up a horn of salvation for us.

INTERCESSIONS

Jesus, tax collectors and public sinners experienced your
goodness and changed their lives;
  —help us to enable others to grow and realize their worth.
You had compassion on the weak and sorrowful;
  —open our eyes and hearts to the ways we can comfort others.
You were a gift to all who came to you in faith;
  —fill us with love that is creative and fruitful for your people
  and the world.
No one is beyond the reach of your care;
  —bless those in refugee camps and all who are uprooted from
  their homes and land.
Make us wise as serpents and simple as doves;
  —make us a people after your own heart.

PRAYER: All loving God, let us know your presence as we begin
this day. Guide us as we strive to choose what is good
and just. Lift up our hearts to you when the demands
of the day threaten to lead us astray. This we ask

through Jesus who is our way, our truth and our life. Amen.

DAYTIME PRAYER

Ant. 1 Blessed are they who hear your word and keep it.

Psalm 119:49–56

Remember your word to your
servant,
by which you gave me hope.
This is my comfort in my affliction
that your promise gives me life.

Though the proud utterly deride
me,
I do not turn from your law.
When I think of your precepts of
old,
I take comfort, O God.

I am seized with indignation
because of the wicked,
who forsake your law.
Your statutes have been my songs
in the house of my pilgrimage.

I remember your name in the night,
and keep your law.
This blessing has been given to me,
the keeping of your precepts.
    Glory*...

Ant. 2 You free us from the bondage of sin and restore us to life.

Psalm 53

Fools say in their hearts:
"There is no God."
They are corrupt, doing wicked
things;
there are none that do good.

God looks down from heaven
on the peoples of the earth,—

to see if any are wise,
if any seek God.

They have all fallen away;
they are all alike depraved;
there are none that do good,
no, not even one.

Have the evildoers no
understanding,
who eat up my people just as they
eat bread,
and do not call upon God?

There they are, in great terror,
such terror as has not been!
For God will chastise the
oppressors;
they will be put to shame.

O that salvation might come from
Zion!
When you restore the fortunes of
your people,
Jacob will rejoice and Israel be
glad. **Glory*...**

Ant. 3 O God, my eyes rejoice in your salvation.

Psalm 54:1–6, 8–9

Save me, O God, by your name;
deliver me by your might.
O God, hear my prayer;
give ear to the words of my mouth.

For the insolent have risen against
me,
the ruthless seek my life;
they set themselves before you.
But I have you for my helper;
You uphold my life.

With a willing heart I make
  sacrifice;
and give thanks to your name.—

You deliver me from all trouble,
my eyes rejoice in your salvation.
  Glory*...

PRAYER: O God, you sent your son, Jesus, to call us to your
realm of mercy and love. Let our memories of his words
and deeds overflow into our lives, that following him,
we may lead others to salvation. We ask this through
the intercession of all those who lived as true disciples
and now live eternally with you. Amen.

EVENING PRAYER

**Ant. 1 Our riches lie in the glory
of God.**

Psalm 49

Hear this, all you peoples!
Give heed, all dwellers of the world,
you, both low and high,
rich and poor together!

My lips will speak words of wisdom;
my heart will ponder your ways.
I will incline my ear to a proverb;
I will solve my riddle on the lyre.

Why should I fear in times of
  trouble,
when the malice of my foes
  surrounds me,
those who trust in their wealth,
and boast of the vastness of their
  riches?

For we cannot buy our own
  ransom,
or give to God the price for our
  lives.
The ransom of our lives is beyond
  us.
It can never be enough,
to avoid going to the grave.

Both the wise and the foolish must
  perish—

and leave their wealth to others.
Their graves are their homes
  forever,
their dwelling places to all
  generations,
though their names spread wide
  through the land.
They are like the beasts that
  perish. **Glory*...**

**Ant. 2 Be not afraid, I go before
you.**

II

This is the fate of those with foolish
  confidence,
the end of those who are pleased
  with their portion.
Like sheep they are driven to the
  grave;
death shall be their shepherd;
straight to the grave they descend,
and their form shall waste away;
the grave shall be their home.

But you will ransom my soul from
  the power of the grave,
for you will receive me.

Be not afraid when people grow
  rich,
when the glory of their houses
  increases.—

They carry nothing with them when
  they die,
their glory will not go down with
  them.

Though while they lived, they
  thought themselves happy,
and thought themselves praised for
  their success,
they will go to join their ancestors,
who will never more see the light.

People cannot abide in insolence;
they are like the beasts that perish.
  Glory*...

**Ant. 3 Worthy is the Lamb who
  was slain.**
  Cant: Rev 4:11, 5:9, 10, 12

Worthy are you, O God, our God,
to receive glory and honor and
  power.

For you have created all things;
by your will they came to be and
  were made.

Worthy are you to take the scroll
  and to open its seals,
For you were slain, and by your
  blood,
you purchased for God
saints of every race and tongue,
of every people and nation.

You have made of them a kindom,
and priests to serve our God,
and they shall reign on the earth.

Worthy is the Lamb who was slain
to receive power and riches,
wisdom and strength,
honor and glory and praise.
  Glory*...

READING

RESPONSORY

Your compassion, O God, calls us to repentance.—**Your...**
Your love heals us, and —**call us...**
Glory to you, Source of all Being, Eternal Word and Holy Spirit.
  —**Your...**

CANTICLE OF MARY

Ant. My spirit rejoices in God, my Savior.

INTERCESSIONS

Eternal God, you create us and call us to realize our union with
you;
  —help us to rise above all that undermines our calling.
Jesus, you were called a fool for our sake;
  —let us bear the inevitable humiliations of life with
  equanimity.

You brought joy and a new beginning to those who received you;
 —give us a hunger for your presence and your truth.
Spirit of God, your realm of love encompasses all of creation;
 —in times of temptation and doubt, draw us ever closer to you.
Your love is eternal;
 —bless and heal those who are burdened with hatred or
 unforgiveness.

PRAYER: Spirit of God, promise of Jesus, come to our help at
the close of this day. Come with forgiveness and
healing love. Come with light and hope. Come with all
that we need to continue in the way of your truth. So
may we praise you in the Trinity forever. Amen.

WEDNESDAY

MORNING PRAYER

**Ant 1 You, O God, are faithful;
all your ways are holy.**

Psalm 77

I cry aloud to you, my God,
cry aloud that you may hear me.

In the day of my trouble I seek
 you,
in the night I stretch out my hand
 without tiring;
my soul refuses to be consoled.

I remember you and I moan;
I ponder, and my spirit faints.
You hold my eyelids from closing;
I am so troubled, I cannot speak.

I consider the days of old,
I remember the years long past.
I converse with my heart in the
 night;
I ponder and search my spirit:

"God, will you spurn us forever,
and never again show us favor?
Has your love vanished forever?—

Are your promises at an end for
 all time?
Have you forgotten to be
 gracious?
Has your anger withheld your
 compassion?"

I say: "This is the cause of my
 grief;
that the way of the Most High has
 changed."
I will call to mind your deeds;
I will remember your wonders of
 old,
I will meditate on all your works,
and ponder your mighty deeds.

Your ways, O God, are holy.
What god is great as our God?
You are the God who works
 wonders,
who shows your power among the
 peoples.
Your strong arm redeemed your
 people,—

the descendants of Jacob and
   Rachel.

When the waters saw you, O God,
when the waters saw you, they
   were afraid,
the depths were moved with
   terror.
The clouds poured out water;
the skies gave forth thunder;
your arrows flashed to and fro.

Your thunder crashed in the
   whirlwind;
your flashes lighted up the world;
the earth trembled and shook.
Your way was through the sea,
your path through the great
   waters;
yet your footprints were not seen.

You led your people like a flock
by the hands of Moses and
   Miriam. **Glory*...**

**Ant. 2 My heart exults in God,
   the joy of my salvation.
      Cant: 1 Samuel 2:1–10**

My heart exults in the Most High,
my strength is exalted in my God.
My lips renounce all that is evil,
because I rejoice in your
   salvation.

There is no Holy One like You;
there is no Rock like our God.
Speak no longer so boastfully,
nor let arrogance come from your
   mouth.
For God is a God of knowledge,
a God who weighs our deeds.

The bows of the mighty are
   broken,
but the feeble are circled with
   strength.—

The full hire themselves out for
   bread,
while the hungry cease to
   hunger.
The barren have borne seven
   children,
but those who have many are
   forlorn.

O God, you put to death and give
   life;
you cast down to the grave and
   raise up.
You make poor and make rich;
you bring low, you also exalt.

You raise up the poor from the
   dust;
you lift the needy from the ash
   heap,
to seat them with those of renown
and inherit a seat of honor.

For the pillars of the earth are
   yours,
on them you set the world.
You will guard the steps of your
   faithful ones,
but wickedness shall perish in
   darkness.
For not by strength shall we
   prevail.

Against evil you will thunder on
   high.
You will judge the ends of the
   earth;
you will give strength to just
   leaders
and exalt the power of your
   anointed ones! **Glory*...**

**Ant. 3 Rejoice, our God comes
to save us.**
Psalm 97

You reign over all; let the earth
  rejoice;
let the many coastlands be glad!
Clouds and thick darkness are
  round about you;
righteousness and justice the
  foundation of your throne.

Fire goes before you,
burning up all that is evil.
Your lightnings lighten the world,
the earth sees and trembles.

Mountains melt like wax before
  you,
before you, Creator of all the
  earth.
The heavens proclaim your
  justice;
all peoples behold your glory.

All who pay homage to idols,
who boast in worthless gods,
are put to shame.
All gods bow down before you.

Zion hears and is glad;
the people of Judah rejoice,
because of your judgments, O
  God.
For you are most high over all the
  earth;
exalted far above all gods.

You love those who hate evil;
you preserve the lives of your
  saints;
you deliver them from
  wickedness.

Light dawns for the just
and joy for the upright of heart.
Rejoice in God, you that are just,
and give thanks to God's holy
  name. **Glory*...**

READING

RESPONSORY

O God, you are One, you love the singlehearted. **—O God,...**
The pure of heart shall see you; **—you love...**
Glory to you, Source of all Being, Eternal Word and Holy Spirit.
  —O God,...

CANTICLE OF ZECHARIAH

Ant. Deliver us, O God, from all that is evil.

INTERCESSIONS

O God, you have made a covenant of love with us;
  —dispel from our minds and hearts the fear that belies your
    care for us.
You have hidden yourself in every blade of grass and every
towering mountain;
  —give us eyes to see your creative love at work in our world.

Jesus, you responded to women with affirmation and love;
  —show us how to encourage and support women when
  others would prevent them from serving you.
You allowed the words of Scripture to form you and to guide your
life;
  —let the word of your life be the foundation of all we do and the
  guide for our lives.
Spirit of God, you are the very life of the church;
  —invade us all with the wisdom, fortitude, and generosity to be
  the people of God in deed and truth.

PRAYER: O God, our Creator, each morning we praise the
wonder of your love. Your tender care measures our
strength and calls us to grow. You give us courage
before the challenge of the day. O Eternal God, make
us worthy of the time you have given us. This we ask
for ourselves and for all of creation through Jesus, our
brother and friend. Amen.

DAYTIME PRAYER

**Ant. 1 Be gracious to me
according to your promise.
Psalm 119:57–64**

You, O God, are my portion;
I promise to obey your words.
I entreat your favor with all my
  heart;
be gracious to me according to
  your promise.

When I think of your ways,
I turn my feet to your will;
I hasten and do not delay
to keep your commandments.

Though the cords of the wicked
  ensnare me
I do not forget your law.
At midnight I rise to praise you,
because of your just decrees.

I am a friend of all who revere
  you,—

of those who obey your precepts.
The earth is full of your steadfast
  love;
teach me your statutes.
    Glory*...

**Ant. 2 Shelter me in the shadow
of your wings.
Psalm 55:1–19, 22–24**

O God, give ear to my prayer;
hide not from my supplication!
attend to me and answer me;
I am overcome by my troubles.

I am distraught by the lure of
  corruption,
at oppression caused by
  wickedness.
The evil that brings trouble upon
  me,
and whose anger weighs on my
  soul.

My heart is in anguish within me,
the terrors of death fall upon me.
Fear and trembling come upon
me,
and horror overwhelms me.

O that I had wings like a dove!
I would fly away and be at rest;
indeed, I would wander afar,
I would take refuge in the
wilderness,
I would haste to find me a shelter
from the raging wind and
tempest.

Overthrow this oppression, O
God,
confuse all who seek to destroy.
For I see violence and strife all
around me.
Day and night it patrols our
cities;
They are full of wickedness and
evil,
ruin is in their midst;
oppression and fraud do not
depart
from their market places.
    Glory*...

**Ant. 3 Let us walk together in
the ways of our God.**
                II

It is not our enemies who cause
this;
then I might bear it;
it is not our foes who oppress,
I might hide from them.

But it is ourselves, our
companions,
our familiar and intimate friends.
We used to speak together of
justice;
We walked together in
companionship in the ways of
our God.

I will call out to you, O God,
and you will save me.
Evening, morning and at noon
I utter complaint and lament;
you will hear my voice.

You will deliver my soul in safety
in the attack waged all around;
for many things can bring me
down,
but you will hear my cry.

You will give ear, and chastise us,
you, who reign from of old;
because we have not kept your
law,
and have not revered you.

Cast your burdens on our God,
and you will be supported.
Never will God permit
the just ones to falter.

But you, O God, will bring down
to the pit of the grave,
all that is wicked and evil;
that oppresses the poor and the
needy.

O God, we will trust in you.
    Glory*...

PRAYER: O God, our daily burdens weigh us down and fear for
our future is no stranger to us. Help us to remember
the life and death of Jesus, that strengthened by his
hope, we, too, may become totally open to your will.
Grant this in Jesus' name. Amen.

EVENING PRAYER

Ant. 1 In silence and stillness, my heart waits for you.
Psalm 62

For God alone my soul waits in
  silence;
From God comes my salvation.
God alone is my rock and my
  stronghold,
my fortress; I shall not be moved.

How long will you set upon me
to break me down,
as though I were a leaning wall,
or a tottering fence?

They only plan to destroy.
They take pleasure in falsehood.
They bless with their mouths,
but inwardly they curse.

For God alone my soul waits in
  silence,
for my hope comes from the Most
  High.
God alone is my rock and my
  stronghold,
my fortress; I shall not be moved.

In you alone is my deliverance,
my mighty rock, my refuge.
We trust in you at all times
and pour out our hearts before
  you;
for you are our refuge.

Common folk are but a breath,
great persons are a delusion.
Placed on the scales, they go up;
together they are lighter than a
  breath.

Put no confidence in extortion,
set no vain hopes on robbery;
do not set your heart on riches,
even if they should increase.

Once God has spoken; twice have
  I heard this:
that power belongs to God;
and to you, O God, steadfast love.
For you repay us according to our
  deeds. **Glory*...**

Ant. 2 Your spirit, O God, moves upon the face of the earth.
Psalm 67

O God, be gracious to us and
  bless us
and make your face shine upon
  us.
That your ways be known upon
  earth,
your saving power among all
  nations.
Let the peoples praise you, O
  God;
let all the peoples praise you.

Let the nations be glad and sing
  for joy,
for you judge the peoples with
  equity
and guide the nations on earth.
Let the peoples praise you, O
  God;
let all the peoples praise you.

The earth has yielded its
  increase;
God, our God, has blessed us.
You, indeed, have blessed us;
let all the earth revere you!
  Glory*...

Ant. 3 You are God's temple; God's spirit dwells in you.
Cant: Colossians 1:12–20

Let us give thanks to God
for having made us worthy—

to share the inheritance of the
saints in light.

God has delivered us
from the power of darkness
and transferred us
into the kindom of God's beloved
Son, Jesus,
in whom we have redemption,
the forgiveness of our sins.

Jesus is the image of the invisible
God,
the first-born of all creation;
in him all things were created,
in heaven and on earth,
things visible and invisible.

All things were created through
him;—

all were created for him.
He is before all else that is.
In him all things hold together.

He is the head of the body, the
church!
He is the beginning,
the firstborn from the dead,
that in everything, he might be
above all others.

In him all the fullness of God was
pleased to dwell,
and through him, to reconcile all
things to himself,
whether on earth or in heaven,
making peace by the blood of his
cross. **Glory*...**

READING

RESPONSORY

You love the poor, O God; you feed them with your word.
   —You love...
They call to you for life; **—you feed...**
Glory to you, Source of all Being, Eternal Word and Holy Spirit.
   —You love...

CANTICLE OF MARY

Ant. Most holy be your name.

INTERCESSIONS

O God, you long to draw us to yourself in a realm of peace;
   —bless all who struggle with relationships in the home and in
   the workplace.
Your gift of faith to us grows by use and for the asking;
   —make us aware of this treasure; let us taste and share its
   fruits.
Jesus, you knew the sins of your followers, but you forgave and
encouraged them in the way of love;
   —let our awareness of our faults lead us to encourage one
   another to turn to you.

You eased the burdens of so many by healing their sickness and wounds;
—give nurses and doctors the skill and compassion they need to do the same.
The alien and stranger are dear to your heart;
—give us the humility and generosity to welcome those who are different from us.

PRAYER: O God, we live in constant need. To whom shall we go but to you? You are both father and mother to us, tending our days with delicate care. We thank you for your love and mercy this day, and we ask you to help us to forgive as we have been forgiven; to give as we have received. This we, your children, ask of you in your tender mercy. Amen.

THURSDAY

MORNING PRAYER

Ant. 1 I am the vine, you are the branches. The one who abides in me will bear much fruit.
Psalm 80

Give ear, O Shepherd of Israel,
you who lead Joseph like a flock!
You who are enthroned upon the cherubim,
shine before Ephraim, Benjamin and Manasseh!
Stir up your might and come to save us!

Restore us, God of hosts;
let your face shine, that we may be saved.
God of hosts, how long will you be angry
with your people's prayers?
You fed them with the bread of tears,
and gave them tears to drink in full measure.—

You made us the scorn of our neighbors,
our enemies laugh among themselves.

Restore us, God of hosts;
let your face shine, that we may be saved.

You brought a vine out of Egypt;
you drove out the nations to plant it.
You cleared the ground before it;
it took root and filled the land.

The mountains were covered with its shade,
the mighty cedars with its branches;
it sent out its branches to the sea,
and its roots to the Great River.

Then why have you broken down its walls?
so that all who pass by pluck its fruit?—

It is ravaged by the boar of the
  forest,
devoured by the beasts of the field.

Turn again, O God of hosts!
Look down from heaven, and see;
have regard for this vine,
the vine you have planted.
It has been burnt with fire and cut
  down.

Let your hand be on those you
  have chosen,
those you make strong for yourself!
Then we will never forsake you;
give us life, and we will call on your
  name.

Restore us, God of hosts!
let your face shine, that we may be
  saved. **Glory*...**

**Ant. 2 God is the joy of my
salvation.**
    Cant: Isaiah 12:1-6

I will give thanks to you, O God;
for though you were angry with me,
your anger turned away,
and you did comfort me.

Behold, you are my savior;
I will trust, and will not be afraid;
you are my strength and my song,
you have become my salvation.

With joy we will draw water from
  the wells of salvation.
We will say on that day:
"We give you thanks and call upon
  your name;
make known your deeds among the
  nations,
proclaim how exalted is your name.

"We sing our praise to you,
for all your glorious deeds;—

let this be known in all the earth."
Shout, and sing for joy, O people of
  Zion,
for great in your midst
is the Holy One of Israel!
  Glory*...

**Ant. 3 Today if you should hear
God's voice, harden not your
heart.**
    Psalm 81

Sing aloud to God our strength;
shout for joy to the God of our
  people.

Raise a song and sound the
  timbrel,
the sweet-sounding harp and the
  lyre.
Blow the trumpet at the new moon,
when the moon is full on our feast.

For this is a statute for Israel,
a command of our God.
Who made it a decree with Joseph,
when he went against the land of
  Egypt.

A voice I had not known said to me:
"I relieved your shoulder of the
  burden;
your hands were freed from the
  basket.
In distress you called, and I
  delivered you;
I answered you, concealed in the
  storm cloud,
I tested you at the waters of
  Meribah.

Hear, O my people, while I
  admonish you!
O Israel, if only you would listen to
  me!
There shall be no strange god
  among you;

You shall not worship an alien god.
I am the Most High, your God,
who brought you up out of the land
    of Egypt.
Open wide your mouth, and I will
    fill it.

But my people did not listen to my
    voice;
Israel would have none of me.
So I gave them over to their
    stubborn hearts,
to follow their own counsels.

O that my people would listen to
    me,
that Israel would walk in my ways!
I would soon subdue their
    enemies,
and turn my hand against their
    foes.

I would feed you with the finest
    wheat,
and with honey from the rock I
    would fill you." **Glory*...**

READING

RESPONSORY

O God, you promise life eternal, asking only that we love.—**O God...**
You are kind to the brokenhearted; —**asking...**
Glory to you, Source of all Being, Eternal Word and Holy Spirit.
    —**O God...**

CANTICLE OF ZECHARIAH

Ant. Let us serve our God in holiness.

INTERCESSIONS

O God, only you know the whole truth about us and our deeds;
    —guide us with your wisdom and compassion in our
    relationships with one another.
Every person and thing that you have created is precious to you;
    —bless those who are handicapped and all who assist them.
Jesus, you crossed the sea and encountered its dangers;
    —bless sailors and all who travel the waters of our world.
We know the story of your life, O Christ, yet mystery abounds;
    —let our search for truth keep us open to the inspiration of the
    Holy Spirit.
Spirit of God, joy is among your many gifts to us;
    —bless artists of every kind—all who lift up our hearts and fill
    the world with beauty and light.

PRAYER: God of the universe, you speak to us in all of creation,
    but you call to us most surely in the depths of our
    hearts. Help us to listen for your voice today, gentling

our work, our recreation, and our relationships with others in ways that let us hear you. Deepen in us our faith in your presence to us. Grant this through the intercession of all your prophets who listened in sincerity and truth. Amen.

DAYTIME PRAYER

Ant. 1 Teach me discernment that I may know your ways.
Psalm 119:65–72

You have been good to your servant,
according to your word, O God.
Teach me discernment and knowledge,
for I trust in your commands.

Before I was afflicted I went astray;
but now I keep your word.
You are good and your deeds are good;
teach me your commandments.

The proud smear me with lies,
yet I keep your precepts.
Their hearts are closed to good
but I delight in your law.

It was good for me to be afflicted,
that I might learn your statutes.
The law of your mouth is better to me
than silver and gold. **Glory*...**

Ant. 2 Take heart, it is I; have no fear.
Psalm 56:1–7b, 9–14

Be gracious to me, O God,
some there are who crush me;
they trample upon me all day long,
for many fight proudly against me.

When I am afraid,
I put my trust in you.—

In you, whose word I praise,
In you I trust without fear.
What can mortal flesh do to me?

All day long they injure my cause,
all their thoughts are for evil.
They band together, they lurk,
they watch my steps.

You have kept count of my wanderings;
you have kept a record of my tears!
Are they not written in your book?
Then my foes will be turned back
in the day when I call to you.

This I know, that God is with me.
In God, whose word I praise,
in the Holy One, whose word I praise,
in God I trust without a fear.
What can mortal flesh do to me?

My vows to you I will make, O God.
I will render you thanks.
For you delivered my soul from death,
my feet from falling,
that I may walk before you
in the light of life. **Glory*...**

Ant. 3 My heart is steadfast; I will praise you all my days.
Psalm 57

Have mercy on me, have mercy,
for in you my soul takes refuge.—

In the shadow of your wings I take
  refuge
till the storms of destruction pass
  by.

I cry to God the Most High,
to God who has always been my
  help.
May you send from heaven and
  save me
and shame those who trample
  upon me.
O God, send your truth and your
  love.

My soul lies down among lions,
who greedily devour the peoples of
  the earth.
Their teeth are spears and arrows,
their tongues sharpened swords.

Be exalted, O God, above the
  heavens;
let your glory be over all the earth!

They laid a snare for my steps,
my soul was bowed down.
They dug a pit in my path
but they fell in it themselves.

My heart is steadfast, O God,
my heart is steadfast.
I will sing and make melody!
Awake, my soul,
awake, lyre and harp!
I will awake the dawn!

I will give thanks to you among the
  peoples,
I will praise you among the nations
for your love reaches to the
  heavens
your faithfulness to the skies.

Be exalted, O God, above the
  heavens!
let your glory be over all the earth!
  Glory*...

PRAYER: O God, you bless those who hunger and thirst for
justice. We ask for the gift of this desire. Imprint on our
minds and in our hearts the longings of your son,
Jesus, that our labor this day may be done justly and
that we too may bless those who labor for the sake of
justice. This we ask in Jesus who is our Way, our
Truth, and our Life. Amen.

EVENING PRAYER

**Ant. 1 You are the salt of the
earth; you are the light of the
world.**

Psalm 72

Give justice to your Anointed, O
  God,
and righteousness to those
  Chosen!
That your people may be judged in
  righteousness,
and your poor with justice.

Let the mountains bring forth
  peace for the people,
and the hills, justice!
May your Anointed
defend the cause of the poor,
give deliverance to the needy,
and punish the oppressor!

May your Anointed endure like the
  sun,
and as long as the moon, through
  all ages,—

like rain that falls on the mown
   grass,
like showers that water the earth.

In that day justice shall flourish
and peace till the moon be no
   more!
Your Anointed shall rule from sea
   to sea,
from the River to the ends of the
   earth!

May evil bow down before the Holy
   One,
and wickedness lick the dust!
The kings of Tarshish and of the
   isles shall render tribute.

May rulers of Sheba and Seba
   bring gifts.
All will fall down before the
   Anointed,
all nations serve and pay homage.
   Glory*...

**Ant. 2 God will save the poor
   from oppression and violence.
         II**

The Anointed delivers the needy
   when they call,
the poor and those who are
   helpless.
Having pity on the weak and the
   needy,
saving the lives of the poor.

From oppression and violence they
   are redeemed;
and precious is their blood.
Long may your Chosen One live,
may gold of Sheba be given
to the one you have anointed,
and prayers be made without
   ceasing,
and blessings all the day!

May there be abundance of grain in
   the land,
waving on the tops of the
   mountains;
may its fruit be like Lebanon;
may people flourish in the cities
like the grass in the field!

May the name of your Anointed
   endure forever,
and continue as long as the sun!
Every tribe shall be blessed in the
   one you have chosen,
all nations bless your name.

Blessed be the God of Israel,
who alone does wondrous things.
Blessed be your name forever;
may your glory fill the earth.
Amen! Amen!   **Glory*...**

**Ant. 3 Lamb of God, you take
   away the sin of the world.
      Cant: Rev 11:17–18;
            12:10b–12a**

We praise you, God Almighty,
who is and who was.
You have assumed your great
   power,
you have begun your reign.

The nations have raged in anger,
but then came your day of wrath
and the moment to judge the dead;
the time to reward your servants
   the prophets
and the holy ones who revere you,
the great and the small alike.

Now have salvation and power
   come,
your reign, O God, and the
   authority of your Anointed One.
For the accusers of our loved ones
   have been cast out,
who night and day accused them.

By the blood of the Lamb have they
been defeated,
and by the testimony of your
servants;— love for life did not deter them from
death.
So rejoice, you heavens,
and you that dwell therein!
Glory*...

READING

RESPONSORY

You are bountiful, O God; all of your desires for us are good.
—**You...**
Everything is a grace; —**all of...**
Glory to you, Source of all Being, Eternal Word and Holy Spirit.
—**You...**

CANTICLE OF MARY

**Ant. You have shown your power, O God; you have scattered
the proud in their hearts' fantasy.**

INTERCESSIONS

You hear our prayers and guide and protect us, O God;
—be praised and thanked for all that we take for granted and
for hidden gifts.
You offer us the grace to become a new person in Christ;
—in times of boredom, awaken us to the world of the Spirit we
so often ignore.
Jesus, you were content to hide your glory and to give in secret;
—strengthen our inward self that we may find our true peace
beyond the measure of others.
You challenged the status quo; you died for being different;
—give courage and peace to all who live on the fringes of society.
You promised a peace that the world cannot give;
—banish war from our world.

PRAYER: Jesus, our Savior and Guide, you gave yourself to us
through a meal at the end of a day, at the end of your
life. Be with us at the end of this day as we dedicate
ourselves to all that you call us to be. Help us to say to
God with you, "Thy will be done." Let us conclude this
day strengthened by the remembrance of your total gift
of self. We ask this through the power of your name.
Amen.

FRIDAY

MORNING PRAYER

Ant 1 A contrite heart, O God, is pleasing in your sight.
Psalm 51

Have mercy on me, O God,
according to your steadfast love;
in your abundant mercy blot out
  my sins.
Wash me thoroughly from my
  offenses,
and cleanse me from my sin!

For I know my offenses,
and my sin is ever before me.
Against you, you alone, have I
  sinned,
and done what is evil in your
  sight,
so you are justified in your
  sentence
and blameless in your judgment.
Behold, I was brought forth in a
  sinful world.

For you desire truth in my
  innermost being;
teach me wisdom in the depths of
  my heart.
O purify me, and I shall be clean;
O wash me, I shall be whiter than
  snow.
Fill me with joy and gladness;
let the bones you have broken
  rejoice.
Hide your face from my guilt,
and blot out all my offenses.

Create in me a clean heart,
put a steadfast spirit within me.
Cast me not from your presence,
take not your spirit from me.
Give me again the joy of your
  salvation,
with a willing spirit uphold me.

Then I will teach transgressors
  your ways,
and sinners will return to you.
Deliver me from death,
O God of my salvation,
and my tongue will sing out your
  saving help.

Open my lips and my mouth will
  sing your praises.
For you take no delight in
  sacrifice;
were I to give a burnt offering,
you would not be pleased.
A broken spirit you accept;
a contrite heart, you will not
  despise.

In your goodness, show favor to
  Zion;
rebuild the walls of Jerusalem.
Then you will delight in just
  sacrifices,
in gifts offered on your altar.
   Glory*...

Ant. 2 Your mercy reaches to the heavens; your mercy covers the earth.
Cant: Habakkuk 3:2–4, 13a, 15–19

O God, I have heard your renown,
and your work, O God, do I
  revere.
In the course of the years renew
  it;
in the course of the years make it
  known;
in your wrath remember mercy!

God came from Teman,
and the Holy One from Mount
  Paran.—

Your glory covered the heavens,
O God,
and the earth was full of your
praise.

Your brightness was like the
light,
rays flashed forth from your
hand;
there you veiled your power.
You went forth to save your
people,
for the salvation of your anointed.

You trampled the sea with your
horses,
the surging of mighty waters.
I hear, and my body trembles,
my lips quiver at the sound.

Decay enters my bones,
my legs totter beneath me.
I wait for the day of trouble
to come on those who oppress us.
   Glory*...

**Ant. 3 Hear the word of God, O
people.**
         Psalm 147:12-20

O praise the Most High,
Jerusalem!
Praise your God, O Zion!

For God strengthens the bars of
your gates,
blessing your children within
you,
establishing peace in your
borders,
feeding you with the finest of
wheat.

You send out your word to the
earth;
your command runs swiftly,
giving snow like wool,
scattering hoarfrost like ashes.

You cast forth your ice like
crumbs;
who can stand before your cold?
You send forth your word, and
melt them;
you make the wind blow, and the
waters flow.

You make your word known to
your people,
your statutes and decrees to
Israel.
You have not dealt thus with any
other nation;
you have not taught them your
decrees. **Glory*...**

READING

RESPONSORY

Who will deliver us, O God, from our weakness and sin?
   —Who will...
Jesus Christ has saved us **—from our...**
Glory to you, Source of all Being, Eternal Word and Holy Spirit.
   —Who will...

CANTICLE OF ZECHARIAH

**Ant. You are compassionate, O God, and forever faithful to
   your promise.**

INTERCESSIONS

O God, you have created us for what eye has not seen and ear has
not heard;
—give us open minds and largeness of heart that we may see
and serve beyond ourselves.

Jesus, you served and saved others—ridicule did not shrink your
compassion;
—make us singlehearted in our care for others.

With religious authority against you and disciples slow to
understand, you stayed your course to the end;
—give perseverance to the new and creative in our culture,
that your message may live on in us.

Jesus, you knew the innocence and vulnerability of childhood;
—guide and protect the children of our disturbed and violent
world.

Spirit of God, you promote progress, you make all things new;
—give us the vision we need to develop for the better without
destroying our vital heritage.

PRAYER: O God, your son, Jesus, died giving the message of
your love to us. Have mercy on us. Give us the courage
to die rather than cause the death of another. Help us
to allow his death to mean new life for us. Never let us
stand in the way of your saving grace. Grant this
through the intercession of Jesus and all who have
given their lives for others. Amen.

DAYTIME PRAYER

**Ant. 1 Blessed be God who
comforts us in all our
affliction.**
Psalm 119:73–80

Your hands have made me and
have fashioned me;
give me understanding that I may
learn your commandments.
Those who revere you will see me
and rejoice,
because I have hoped in your
word.

I know that your judgments are
right,
that in faithfulness you afflicted
me.
Let your love be ready to comfort
me
according to your promise.

Let your mercy come to me, that I
may live;
for your law is my delight.
Let the godless be put to
shame,—

who have corrupted me with
  guile,
while I will ponder on your
  precepts.

Let those who revere you turn to
  me,
that they may know your will.
May my heart be blameless in
  your commandments,
that I may not be put to shame!
  Glory*...

**Ant. 2 We have a treasure in
earthen vessels, to show the
power of God.**
  Psalm 59:1–5, 10–11, 17–18

Deliver me from evil, O my God,
protect me from those who
  oppress me,
deliver me from all that is wicked,
and save me from all cruelty.

Calamity lies in wait for my life;
misfortune bands together
  against me.
For no offense or sin of mine,
for no fault, they run and make
  ready.
Rouse yourself, come to my aid
  and see!

O my Strength, I will sing praises
  to you;
for you, O God, are my
  stronghold.
In your steadfast love you will
  meet me;
O God, come to my aid,
let me triumph over oppression.

As for me, I will sing of your
  might;
each morning sing of your love.
For you have been to me a
  stronghold—

and a refuge in the day of
  distress.

O my Strength, I will sing praises
  to you,
for you, O God, are my
  stronghold,
the God who shows me love
  without end.   **Glory*...**

**Ant. 3 Blessed are you, O God;
you heal us while wounding
us.**
  Psalm 60

O God, you have rejected us and
  broken our defenses;
You have turned your face;
  restore us.
You have made the land to quake,
  torn it open;
Repair its breaches for it totters.
You have made your people suffer
  hard things,
and have given us wine that
  made us reel.

You have set up a signal for those
  who fear you,
to rally to it from the bow.
That your faithful ones may be
  delivered,
help us by your hand and give
  answer!

You have spoken from your
  sanctuary:
"With exultation I will divide
  Shechem
and portion out the Vale of
  Succoth.

Gilead is mine and Manasseh;
Ephraim is my helmet,
Judah is my scepter.

Moab is my washbasin;
upon Edom I cast my shoe.—

Over Philistia I will shout in
triumph."

Who will bring me to the fortified
city?
Who will lead me to Edom?
Have you not rejected us, O
God?—

You did not go forth with our
armies.

Give us help against the foe,
for human help is vain.
With you we shall do valiantly;
it is you who will tread down
oppression. **Glory*...**

PRAYER: Lord Jesus Christ, the marvel of your love lives on and
challenges everyone who comes to know you. In you we
know the love of God; through you we know the will
and ways of God. Be with us now that we may live for
one another as you have lived and died for us. Grant
this through your Spirit of Love. Amen.

EVENING PRAYER

**Ant. 1 You are gracious, O God,
and full of compassion.**

Psalm 116:1–9

I love you, O God, for you have
heard
my voice and my supplications.
You have inclined your ear to me,
I will call on you as long as I live.

The snares of death encompassed
me;
the pangs of the grave laid hold
on me;
I suffered distress and anguish.
Then I called on your name, O
God:
"O God, I pray you, save my life!"

Gracious are you and just;
merciful and full of compassion.
You preserve those with simple
hearts;
when I was brought low, you
saved me.

Return my soul, to your rest;
for God has dealt kindly with you,
delivering my soul from death,
my eyes from tears,
my feet from stumbling.

I will walk before you, O God,
in the land of the living.
Glory*...

**Ant. 2 God is my comforter and
help in time of need.**
Psalm 121

I lift up my eyes to the hills.
From whence comes my help?
My help comes from you, O God,
who made heaven and earth.

You will not let my foot stumble,
you, who preserve me, will not
sleep.
Behold, you who keep Israel
will neither slumber nor sleep.

You, O God, are our keeper;
you are our shade.
The sun shall not smite us by
  day,
nor the moon by night.

You will guard us from all evil;
you will preserve our lives.
You will protect our goings and
  comings
both now and forever.
  Glory*...

**Ant. 3 Ruler of all the ages, just
and true are your ways.**

Cant: Rev 15:3–4

Great and wonderful are your
  works,
God the Almighty One!
Just and true are your ways,
Ruler of all the ages!

Who shall refuse you honor,
or the glory due your name?

For you alone are holy,
all nations shall come and
  worship in your presence.
Your judgments are clearly seen.
  Glory*...

READING

RESPONSORY

Lord Jesus Christ, your yoke is easy and your burden is light.
  —Lord Jesus...
In you we will find rest; **—for your yoke...**
Glory to you, Source of all Being, Eternal Word and Holy Spirit.
  —Lord Jesus...

CANTICLE OF MARY

**Ant. You put down the mighty from their throne and lift up
the lowly.**

INTERCESSIONS

Jesus, you washed the feet of your followers;
  —teach all civic and religious leaders how to govern with
  humility and reverence.
You did not call your disciples servants but friends;
  —help us to establish your kindom by mutual collaboration and
  loving respect.
You shared a meal with one who had betrayed you;
  —give us the desire to set aside our mistrust of one another.
Jesus, you came into the world to testify to the truth;
  —make us credible witnesses to the truth of your gospel.

You suffered at the hands of those you served;
—enable us to serve one another selflessly without regard for
human success.

PRAYER: Holy Spirit, Living Love of God, you are in the world
healing the wounds of sin and death. Warm the hearts
of those embittered by sorrow and pain, encourage
those crushed by failure, enlighten the minds of those
dulled by pleasure or fatigue. Awaken in us all the
remembrance of the overwhelming love of God made
known to us in the life and death of Jesus. Help us to
continue with renewed trust. This we ask of you, Life-
giving Spirit, in the name of your Christ, God among
us. Amen.

SATURDAY

MORNING PRAYER

**Ant. 1 We acclaim your love in
the morning and your
faithfulness at night.**
Psalm 92

It is good to give thanks to you,
to sing praises to your name, Most
High,
to declare your love in the morning,
and your faithfulness by night,
to the music of the lute and the
harp,
to the melody of the lyre.

For you make me glad by your
deeds;
at the work of your hands I sing for
joy.
How great are your works, O God!
Your thoughts are very deep!

The foolish ones cannot know;
the stupid cannot understand this:
though the wicked spring up like
grass
and all evildoers flourish,—

they are doomed to their own
devices.
But you, O God, are on high
forever.
All wickedness shall perish;
all oppression be wiped out.

You give me the strength of the
wild ox;
you pour oil over my head.
My eyes have seen the downfall of
evil,
my ears have heard the doom of
corruption.
The just shall flourish like the palm
tree
and grow like a cedar in Lebanon.

They are planted in your holy
house,
they flourish in your courts.
They still bring forth fruit in old
age,
they are ever full of sap and green,
to show that you, O God, are
just;—

you are my rock; in you there is no
injustice. **Glory*...**

**Ant. 2 We declare your greatness,
O God.**
Cant: Deut 32:1-12

Give ear, O heavens, while I speak;
let the earth hear the words of my
mouth.
May my teaching soak in like the
rain,
and my speech permeate like the
dew,
like a gentle rain upon the tender
grass,
like a shower upon the herbs.

For I will proclaim your name, O
God.
Declare your holy greatness!
"My Rock, your work is faultless;
all your ways are justice.
A faithful God, without deceit,
how just and right you are!

Yet basely have you been dealt
with by your sinful children,
a perverse and crooked generation.
Is God to be thus requited,
you foolish and senseless people?
Is God not your source, who
created you,
who made you and established
you?

Remember the days of old,
Consider the years of many
generations;
Ask your parents and they will
inform you,
ask your elders and they will tell
you.

When the Most High gave the
nations their inheritance,—

separating the children of the
earth,
the Most High fixed the boundaries
of the peoples
according to the number of those in
your court.
But your portion, O God, is your
people,
Jacob, your allotted heritage.

You found them in a desert land,
in the howling waste of the
wilderness;
encircling them and caring for
them,
guarding them as the apple of your
eye.

Like an eagle that stirs up its nest,
that flutters over its young,
so you spread your wings to catch
them,
and bear them on your pinions.
You alone were their leader,
no strange god was with our God."
Glory*...

**Ant. 3 How great is your name in
all the earth.**
Psalm 8

How great is your name, O God,
in all the earth!

You whose glory above the heavens
is chanted on the lips of babes,
have founded a defense against
your foes,
to silence the cries of the rebels.

When I look at the heavens,
the work of your hands,
the moon and the stars which you
established;
who are we that you should keep
us in mind,
mortal flesh that you care for us?

Yet you have made us little less than God,
and crowned us with glory and honor.
You entrust us with the works of your hands,
to care for all your creation.

All sheep and oxen,—
and even the beasts of the field,
the birds of the air, and the fish of the sea,
whatever passes along the paths of the sea.

How great is your name, Creator God,
in all the earth! **Glory*...**

READING

RESPONSORY

Those who wait for you, O God, shall never be disappointed.
  —Those who...
They shall see you face to face; **—and shall...**
Glory to you, Source of all Being, Eternal Word and Holy Spirit.
  —Those who...

CANTICLE OF ZECHARIAH

Ant. Guide our feet into the way of peace.

INTERCESSIONS

O God, you know of what we are made, and you give us all that we need;
  —let us mirror your compassion to one another.
Jesus, many dismissed your teaching because of your common origin;
  —help us to look beyond surface impressions to the true value of each person.
Our attachments and addictions lay heavy burdens upon us;
  —teach us how to listen to your freeing word written in our hearts.
You knew rejection and derision;
  —give us the desire to serve all and the grace to be at peace when we cannot please everyone.
Our culture tends to reward the strong and powerful and to dismiss the weak;
  —make all that we do reflect your gospel, your good news to the poor.

PRAYER: Merciful God, we often stray from your call and our own good intentions, but you meet us with forgiveness and creative love. Give us the gift of patience and understanding that we, too, may lure others to new life. May all who die this day enjoy life with you as they see you face to face. Grant this through Mary, who brought new life to us in Jesus. Amen.

DAYTIME PRAYER

Ant. 1 In your love spare my life, that I may keep your decrees.

Psalm 119:81–88

My soul pines for your salvation;
I hope in your word.
My eyes fail with watching for
  your promise;
"When will you comfort me?"

Though parched and exhausted
  with waiting,
I have not forgotten your
  commands.
How long must your servant
  endure?
When will you requite me?

Evil waits to entrap me
to sin against your law.
All your commandments are sure;
then help me when oppressed by
  falsehood!

Death lurks to make an end of
  me;
but I forsake not your precepts.
In your steadfast love spare my
  life,
that I may do your will. **Glory*...**

Ant. 2 O God, you are my refuge, my stronghold against evil.

Psalm 61

Hear my cry, O God,
listen to my prayer;
from the end of the earth I call,
when my heart is faint.

Set me on the rock that is higher
  than I;
for you are my refuge,
my stronghold against evil.

Let me dwell in your tent forever!
Hide me in the shelter of your
  wings!
For you, O God, have heard my
  vows,
you have given me the heritage
of those who love your name.

May you lengthen the lives of just
  rulers:
may their years cover many
  generations!
May they ever be enthroned
  before you;
bid love and truth watch over
  them.

So will I ever sing your praises,
as I pay my vows day after day.
  Glory*...

Ant. 3 O God, preserve my life from corruption.

Psalm 64

Hear my voice, O God, in my
  complaint;
preserve my life from all that is
  evil,
hide me from the tempter's snare,
from the scheming wiles of my
  heart.

Evil sharpens its tongue like a
  sword;
aiming bitter words like arrows,
shooting from ambush at the
  innocent,
shooting suddenly and without
  fear.

Holding fast to its evil purpose;
conspiring to lay secret snares—

thinking: "Who can see us?
Who can search out our crimes?"

But you know well our inmost
  thoughts,
the depth of the heart and mind!
You will shoot your arrow at
  them;
they will be wounded suddenly.
Our own tongues bring us to
  ruin.

Then let all people fear;
they will tell what you have
  wrought,
and ponder what you have done.
The just will rejoice in you, O
  God,
and fly to you for refuge.
Let the upright in heart exult.
  Glory*...

PRAYER: Another week has passed, O God, and we see all that
we have done and what we might have done differently.
We give all of our endeavors to you. Bless the good and
heal the faulty. Inspire us to do your will more
creatively and generously in the week to come. We ask
this through Jesus who shows us the way. Amen.

WEEK III

SUNDAY, EVENING PRAYER I

Ant 1 Your glory is above the heavens; we praise your name.

Psalm 113

We your servants, praise you!
Praise your holy name!
Blessed be your name, O God,
from now and forevermore!
From the rising of the sun to its
setting
your name is to be praised!

You are high above all nations,
and your glory above the
heavens!
Who is like unto you, O God,
who is seated upon the heights,
who looks far down upon us,
upon the heavens and the earth?

You raise the poor from the dust,
lift the needy from the ash heap,
to set them in the company of
rulers,
with the rulers of your people.
To the barren you give a home,
and gladden their hearts with
children. **Glory*...**

Ant 2 I will lift up the cup of salvation and call on your holy name.

Psalm 116:10–19

I kept faith, even when I said:
"I am greatly afflicted;"—

*Glory to you, Source of all Being, Eternal Word and Holy Spirit,

As it was in the beginning is now and will be forever. Amen.

I said in my dismay,
"No one can be trusted."

What shall I render to you,
for all your goodness to me?
I will lift up the cup of salvation
and call on your holy name.

I will make my vows to you
in the presence of all your people.
Precious in your sight
is the death of your faithful ones.

Indeed, I am your servant;
you have loosened my bonds.
I will offer sacrifice of
thanksgiving
and call on your holy name.

I will make my vows to you
in the presence of all your people,
in the courts of your holy house,
in the midst of all your saints.
Glory*...

Ant 3 Every tongue will proclaim: Jesus Christ is Lord!

Cant: Phil 2:6–11

Though he was in the form of
God,
Jesus did not count equality with
God
something to be grasped at.

But emptied himself
taking the form of a slave,
being born in human likeness.

Being found in human estate,
he humbled himself and became
obedient,
obediently accepting death,
even death on a cross!

Therefore God has highly exalted him
and bestowed on him the name above every other name.

So that at the name of Jesus every knee should bow,—

in heaven, on the earth, and under the earth,
and every tongue proclaim to the glory of God:
Jesus Christ is Lord! **Glory*...**

READING

RESPONSORY

We sing to you, O God, and bless your name. **—We sing...**
Tell of your salvation day after day; **—and bless...**
Glory to you, Source of all Being, Eternal Word and Holy Spirit.
   —We sing...

CANTICLE OF MARY

Ant. You have helped your servant, Israel, remembering your mercy.

INTERCESSIONS

O God, you speak to us in many ways;
   —keep us open to your guidance from sources however
      great or humble.
We cherish our call to serve you, and we endeavor to be faithful;
   —deliver us from the plethora of idols that beckon to us
      daily.
Bless all who are united in marriage;
   —let the grace of the sacrament enable them to love and
      support one another.
Jesus, you knew the challenge of choosing your direction in life;
   —send your Spirit to guide those who struggle with
      vocational choices.
Spirit of God, grant wisdom, understanding, and fortitude to all
involved in the media;
   —let the highest values and principles govern their decisions
      and programs.

PRAYER: All holy, ever present God, at the close of this day we
offer to you the world's struggle toward wholeness. We
are confident that our darkness and sin have been
redeemed through the life and death of Jesus and that

your mercy has no limit. Give us the gift of mercy for ourselves and for others. We ask this in Jesus' name. Amen.

MORNING PRAYER

Ant 1 Glory to God in the highest.

Psalm 93

O God, you are our Sovereign,
you are robed in majesty;
you are girded with strength.
The world is made firm;
it shall never be moved;
your throne is established from of old;
from all eternity, you are.

The waters have lifted up, O God,
the waters have lifted up their voice,
the waters have lifted up their thunder.
Mightier than the roaring of the waters,
mightier than the surgings of the sea,
You, O God, are glorious on high!

Your decrees are to be trusted.
Holiness befits your house,
O God, for evermore.
   Glory*...

Ant 2 Praise and exalt God above all, forever.

Cant: Daniel 3:57–88, 56

All you works of God, praise our God.
Praise and exalt God above all forever.
All you angels, sing God's praise,
you heavens and waters above.
Sun and moon, and stars of heaven,—

sing praise with the heavenly hosts.

Every shower and dew, praise our God.
Give praise all you winds.
Praise our God, you fire and heat,
cold and chill—dew and rain.
Frost and chill, praise our God.
Praise God, ice and snow.
Nights and days, sing hymns of praise,
light and darkness,
lightnings and clouds.

Let all the earth bless our God.
Praise and exalt God above all forever.
Let all that grows from the earth give praise,
together with mountains and hills.
Give praise, you springs,
you seas and rivers,
dolphins and all water creatures.
Let birds of the air,
beasts, wild and tame,
together with all living peoples,
praise and exalt God above all forever.

O Israel, praise our God.
Praise and exalt God above all forever.
Give praise, you priests,
servants of the Most High,
spirits and souls of the just.
Holy ones of humble heart,
sing your hymns of praise.
Hannaniah, Azariah, Mishael,
praise our God.—

Praise and exalt God above all
forever.

Let us bless our God, Holy
Mystery,
Source of All Being, Word and
Spirit.
Let us praise and exalt God above
all forever.
Blessed are you, O God, in the
firmament of heaven.
Praiseworthy and glorious and
exalted above all forever.

Ant 3 Praise God from the heavens.
Psalm 148

Praise God from the heavens,
Praise God in the heights!
Praise God, all you angels,
Praise God, you heavenly hosts!

Praise God, sun and moon,
Praise God, shining stars.
Praise God, highest heavens,
and the waters above the heavens!

Let them praise the name of
God,—

who commanded and they were
created.
God established them forever;
fixed their bounds which will not
pass away.

Praise God, all you on earth,
sea monsters and all deeps,
fire and hail, snow and frost,
stormy winds that obey God's
word!

Mountains and all hills,
fruit trees and all cedars!
Beasts, wild and tame,
reptiles and birds on the wing!

All earth's rulers and peoples,
leaders and those of renown!
Young men and women,
the old together with children!

Let us praise your name, O God,
for your name alone is exalted;
your glory above heaven and
earth.

You exalt the strength of your
people,
you are praise for all your saints,
for all the faithful near to you.
Glory*...

READING

RESPONSORY

Our hearts rejoice, O God, in your tender care. **—Our hearts...**
We live in peace; **—in your...**
Glory to you, Source of all Being, Eternal Word and Holy Spirit.
—Our hearts...

CANTICLE OF ZECHARIAH

Ant. You have visited and redeemed your people, O God.

INTERCESSIONS

O God, we are one in you, and all that we do affects the whole;

—make us aware of our power to seed the world with
   good or ill by every thought, word, and deed.
Our hearts are torn by the realization of the sufferings of others;
   —grant that we may never be a stumbling block to others
      or a culpable cause of their pain.
Jesus, you chose laborers, and tax collectors, to be your
companions;
   —preserve us from deciding what people are by what they
      do, and let us see the worth of every person and the
      value in every kind of work.
Bless those who have lost their life companion through death or
divorce;
   —let the people of God be a saving support and comfort to
      them.
Spirit of God, enlighten the minds and renew the hearts of the
hierarchy of the churches;
   —let their ministry be a healing service for all of your people.

PRAYER: God of the universe, you create the night as well as
the day. You are with us in good fortune and bad
times. You order all things for our well being, and you
lure us to truth and holiness. For these and all your
gifts to us we sing your praise through Jesus Christ,
who is our way, our truth and our life. Amen.

DAYTIME PRAYER

**Ant. 1 You are my companion,
   my helper on the way.**
Psalm 118
I

We give thanks to you, for you are
   good,
and your steadfast love endures
   forever.
Let the descendants of Israel say:
"Your steadfast love endures
   forever."
Let the descendants of Aaron say:
"Your steadfast love endures
   forever."
Let those who fear you say:—

"Your steadfast love endures
   forever."

In my distress, I called to you;
you answered me and set me free.
With you at my side I do not fear.
What can anyone do against me?
You are at my side to help me:
I shall withstand all evildoers.

It is better to take refuge in you,
than to trust in people:
it is better to take refuge in you
than to trust in our leaders.
   Glory*...

**Ant. 2 You are my saving God;
you chastise and you bless.**
II

All wickedness surrounded me;
in your name I crushed it.
It surrounded me, surrounded me
   on every side;
in your name I cut it off.
It surrounded me like bees;
it blazed like a fire among thorns.
In your name I crushed it.

I was pushed hard, and was falling
but you came to help me.
You are my strength and my song;
you are my salvation.

O God, you have triumphed;
your reign is exalted.
You have triumphed over all;
I shall not die, I shall live
and recount your wondrous deeds.
You have chastened me sorely,
but have not given me over to
   death. **Glory*...**

**Ant. 3 Blessed is the one who
comes in the name of our God.**
III

Open to me the gates of justice,—

that I may enter and give thanks.
This is your gate, O God;
the just shall enter through it.
I thank you for you have answered
   me;
you alone are my salvation.

The stone which the builders
   rejected
has become the cornerstone.
This is your doing, O God,
it is marvelous in our eyes.
This is the day which you have
   made;
let us rejoice and be glad in it.

Save us, we beseech you, O God!
O God, grant us success.
Blessed are those who enter
in your holy name.
For you O God, are our God,
and you have given us light.

Let us go forward in procession
   with branches,
up to your holy altar.
You are my God, I thank you.
You are my God, I praise you.
We give thanks to you for you are
   good;
and your steadfast love endures
   forever. **Glory*...**

PRAYER: God of mercy, your goodness encompasses the great
and the small. Help us to know your presence in the
most hidden suffering, the most secret pain. Remind
us again of your unfailing love and give us new hope.
This we ask through the intercession of all who
suffered in hope and now live with you. Amen.

EVENING PRAYER II

Ant. 1 God revealed to the Anointed One, "Sit at my side."
Psalm 110:1–5, 7

God's revelation to the Anointed One:
"Sit at my side:
till I put injustice beneath your feet."

God will send forth from Zion
your scepter of power:
rule in the midst of your foes.

Your people will give themselves freely
on the day you lead your host
upon the holy mountains.
From the womb of the morning
your youth will come like dew.

God has sworn an oath that will not be changed.
"You are a priest forever,
after the order of Melchizedek."

The Anointed standing by your side,
will shatter rulers on the day of wrath.

Drinking from your streams by the wayside
shall the Chosen One be refreshed. **Glory*...**

Ant. 2 In your gracious mercy, you cause us to remember your wonderful works.
Psalm 111

I will give thanks to you with all my heart,
in the company of the great assembly.
Great are the works of the Most High;—

pondered by all who delight in them.

Full of honor and majesty is your work,
your justice endures for ever.
You enable us to remember your wonders;
you are gracious and merciful.

You give food to those who fear you;
you are mindful of your covenant.
You have shown your people the power of your works,
by giving them the heritage of the nations.

Your works are faithful and just;
your precepts are all trustworthy,
they are established forever and ever,
to be done in uprightness and truth.

You sent redemption to your people,
and commanded your covenant forever.
Holy and awesome is your name!

To fear you is the beginning of wisdom;
all who do so prove themselves wise.
Your praise endures forever!
Glory*...

Ant. 3 We rejoice and exult in you.
Cant: Rev 19:1, 5–7

Salvation, glory, and power belong to you,
your judgments are honest and true.

All of us, your servants, sing
  praise to you,
we worship you reverently, both
  great and small.
You, our almighty God, are Creator
  of heaven and earth.—

Let us rejoice and exult, and give
  you glory.

The wedding feast of the Lamb has
  begun,
And the bride has made herself
  ready. **Glory*...**

READING

RESPONSORY

You create and sustain us, O God, with your love. **—You...**
From generation to generation **—with your...**
Glory to you, Source of all Being, Eternal Word and Holy Spirit.
  —You...

CANTICLE OF MARY

**Ant. Blessed are you among women and blessed is the fruit of
your womb.**

INTERCESSIONS

Life after death is a mystery to us, O God;
  —let the resurrection of Jesus and his Spirit among us
    witness to your eternal love and care for us.
You ask us to give, to empty ourselves, and to follow you in faith;
  —only to fill us with solid nourishment that enables us to
    live the journey of the gospel.
We know well your law of love; your Spirit lives within us;
  —let no other rule take precedence in our lives.
You came to us bringing peace and reconciliation;
  —may your gospel be the bridge that reconciles us—families,
    communities, and nations.
Bless all who have a great fear of death;
  —grant them peace of heart and friends to support them.

PRAYER: God of wisdom, your steadfast love gives meaning to
our lives. Remembering your goodness from ages past,
we have hope. Our very desire for you is a gift of your
love. Holy Mystery, we do believe; help our unbelief.
This we ask for ourselves, but especially for those
without hope and those who know no love. Hear our
prayer in Jesus' name. Amen.

MONDAY

MORNING PRAYER

Ant 1 My soul is longing for the living God.

Psalm 84

How lovely is your dwelling place,
O God of hosts!

My soul longs and yearns
for the courts of the Most High;
my heart and lips sing for joy
to you, the living God.

Even the sparrow finds a home,
and the swallow a nest for its
  brood,
where it may lay its young,
at your altars, O God of hosts!

Blessed are those who dwell in
  your house,
forever singing your praise!
Blessed are those whose strength
  you are,
in whose hearts are the roads to
  Zion.

As they go through the Bitter
  Valley,
they make it a place of springs;
the early rain covers it with pools.
They go from strength to
  strength;
the God of gods will be seen in
  Zion.

O God of hosts, hear my prayer;
give ear, O God of Jacob!
Look upon our shield, O God;
look on the face of your Anointed!

For one day in your courts is
  better,
than a thousand anywhere else.
I would rather stand at your
  threshold,—

than dwell in the tents of
  wickedness.

For you are a sun and a shield;
you bestow favor and honor.
No good do you withhold
from those who walk uprightly.

O God! God of hosts!
Blessed are those who trust in
  you! **Glory*...**

Ant. 2 Let us walk in your light, O God.
Cant: Isaiah 2:2–5

It shall come to pass in days to
  come,
that the mountain of the house of
  God
shall be established as the
  highest mountain,
and be raised above the hills.

All nations shall flow to it;
many peoples shall come and say:
"Come, let us go up to the
  mountain of God,
to the house of the God of Jacob;
that we may be taught in God's
  ways,
and walk in God's paths."

For from Zion shall go forth the
  law,
and the word of the Most High
  from Jerusalem.
God shall judge between the
  nations,
and shall decide for many
  peoples;
they shall beat their swords into
  plowshares,
and their spears into pruning
  hooks;—

nation shall not lift up sword
against nation,
nor shall they teach war any
more.

O house of Jacob, come,
let us walk in the light of our
God! **Glory*...**

**Ant. 3 Let all things exult in
your presence for you come to
judge the earth.**
Psalm 96

O sing to God a new song;
sing to God, all the earth!
Sing and bless God's name.

We proclaim your salvation day
by day,
declare your glory among the
nations,
your wonders among all the
peoples.

You are great and worthy to be
praised;
to be feared above all gods.
The gods of the nations are idols;
but you made the heavens.
Honor and majesty are before
you;
strength and beauty, in your
sanctuary.

Give to God, you families of
peoples,
give to God glory and power!
Give glory to God's holy name;
bring an offering, and enter God's
courts!
Worship in the temple of the Most
High.
O earth, tremble before the
Almighty.

We proclaim to all nations:
"You, O God, are sovereign.
The world you established:
it shall never be moved;
you will judge the peoples with
equity."

Let the heavens be glad and the
earth rejoice;
let the sea thunder, and all that
fills it;
let the field exult, and everything
in it!
Then shall all the trees of the
wood sing for joy
at your presence, O God, for you
come,
you come to judge the earth.

You will judge the world with
justice,
and the peoples with your truth.
Glory*...

READING

RESPONSORY

There is no limit, O God, to your love for us. **—There is...**
All that you do attests **—to your...**
Glory to you, Source of all Being, Eternal Word and Holy Spirit.
    —There is...

CANTICLE OF ZECHARIAH

Ant. Blessed be the great God of Israel.

INTERCESSIONS

You are our Creator, O God, our lives are in your hands;
  —make us humble and reverent of heart as we unravel
    some small part of the mystery of creation.
Jesus, people were drawn to you for you spoke with authority.
  —bless our public officials with insight for our good, and
    protect them from all that is not just in your sight.
You often spoke to those who were closed to your teaching;
  —give us a contemplative attitude and the grace to
    hear and live your message.
Spirit of God, you hovered over chaos and called forth a world of life;
  —calm us in times of anxiety; teach us how to live one
    moment at a time in your loving presence.
Our hearts are drawn to glorify you, O God, and you receive our humble praise;
  —bless composers, singers and all musicians who enable
    us to express our love and gratitude to you.

PRAYER: O God, we long to follow in the footsteps of Jesus, bringing about your reign of love. Our weakness and sinfulness stop us over and over again. Help us to cooperate with your personal design for each of us and by your strength to embrace your will and to grow in love. Grant this through the intercession of all your saints who inspire, challenge, and call us to the praise of your glory now and forever. Amen.

DAYTIME PRAYER

Ant. 1 I will not forget your precepts; by them you give me life.

Psalm 119:89–96

Forever, O God, your word
is firmly fixed in the heavens.
Your faithfulness endures to all
  generations;
you established the earth,
it will not be moved.

By your decree it stands to this
  day;
for all things are your servants.
If your law had not been my
  delight,
I would have died in my affliction.

I will never forget your precepts;
by them you have given me life.
Save me, for I am yours;
I have sought your precepts.

Wickedness waits to destroy me;
but I ponder your will.
I have seen a limit to all
   perfection,
but your commandment is
   exceedingly broad.
   Glory*...

**Ant. 2 You are my hope; my
   trust from the days of my
   youth.**
Psalm 71

In you, O God, I take refuge;
let me never be put to shame!
In your justice deliver and rescue
   me;
incline your ear to me and save
   me.

Be to me a rock of refuge,
a stronghold to save me,
for you are my rock and my
   stronghold.
Rescue me from the throes of
   oppression,
from the grip of injustice and
   greed.

For you, O God, are my hope,
my trust, O God, from my youth.
Upon you I have leaned from my
   birth;
from my mother's womb you
   claimed me.
I praise you forever and ever.

I have been a portent to many;
but you are my strong refuge.
My lips are filled with your praise,
with your glory all the day.
Do not cast me off in old age;
forsake me not when my strength
   is spent.

O God, be not far from me;
O God, make haste to help me!—

Let evil see its own destruction,
and injustice turn on itself.
   Glory*...

**Ant. 3 Even in old age, O God,
   do not forsake your servant.**
II

But as for me, I will always hope
and praise you more and more.
My lips will tell of your justice,
of your salvation all the day,
for your goodness cannot be
   numbered.

I will declare your mighty deeds,
I will proclaim your justice.
You have taught me from my
   youth,
and I proclaim your wonders still.

Now that I am old and gray-
   headed,
O God, do not forsake me,
till I proclaim your power
to generations to come.
Your power and your justice, O
   God,
reach to the highest heavens.

You have done marvelous things,
O God, who is like you?
You who have made me see many
   sore troubles
will revive me once again;
from the depths of the earth you
   will raise me.
You will exalt and comfort me
   again.

So I will praise you with the harp
for your faithfulness, O God;
I will sing praises to you with the
   lyre,
O Holy One of Israel.

My lips will shout for joy,
when I sing praises to you;—

my soul also, which you have
redeemed.
My tongue will tell of your justice
all the day long,—

PRAYER: Help us, O God, to reach out to those in need. The poor, the elderly, the imprisoned, those who are ill call out to us as they fill out what is wanting in the suffering of Jesus. Give us the wisdom and generosity to minister to them and to manifest your love. Grant this for Jesus' sake who came to set us free. Amen.

EVENING PRAYER

Ant. 1 Our eyes look to you till you have mercy upon us.
Psalm 123

To you I lift up my eyes,
you who are enthroned in the
heavens!
Behold as the eyes of servants
look to the hand of their master,

As the eyes of a maid
look to the hand of her mistress,
so our eyes look to you, O God,
till you have mercy upon us.

Have mercy on us, O God, have
mercy,
for we are filled with contempt.
Too long has our soul been sated
with the scorn of the arrogant,
the contempt of the proud.
        Glory*...

Ant. 2 You will wipe away every tear from our eyes, and death shall be no more.
Psalm 124

If you had not been on our side,
let Israel now say:
if you had not been on our side,—

for evil is put to rout, and all that
sought to harm me.
        Glory*...

when oppression overwhelmed
us,
then would we be swallowed
alive,
when injustice raged against us.

Then the flood would have swept
us away,
the torrent would have gone over
us;
over us would have gone the
raging waters.

Blessed be God who did not give
us
a prey to its teeth!
We have escaped like a bird
from the snare of the fowler;
indeed the snare is broken,
and we have escaped.

Our help is in the name of the
Most High,
who made heaven and earth.
        Glory*...

Ant. 3 O God, you chose us in Jesus to be your children.

Cant: Ephesians 1:3–10

Praised be the God
of our Lord Jesus Christ,—

who has blessed us in Christ
with every spiritual blessing in
the heavens.

God chose us in him
before the foundation of the
world,
that we should be holy
and blameless in God's sight.

We have been predestined
to be God's children through
Jesus Christ,
such was the purpose of God's
will,
that all might praise the glorious
favor
bestowed on us in Christ.

In Christ and through his blood,
we have redemption,
the forgiveness of our sins,
according to the riches of God's
grace lavished upon us.

For God has made known to us
in all wisdom and insight,
the mystery of the plan set forth
in Christ.

A plan to be carried out in Christ,
in the fullness of time,
to unite all things in Christ,
things in heaven and things on
earth. **Glory*...**

READING

RESPONSORY

Your mercy, O God, calls us to mercy. **—Your mercy...**
It manifests your greatness; **—and calls...**
Glory to you, Source of all Being, Eternal Word and Holy Spirit.
    —Your mercy...

CANTICLE OF MARY

Ant. Your regard has blessed me, O God.

INTERCESSIONS

In you, O God, resides all creative energy, and we receive our lives
from you;
    —inspire us with great desires, and let our hope be larger
        than our doubt.
We are a wounded people, afflicted by sin and ignorance;
    —guide and protect our police and all who are missioned
        to protect us; arm them with wisdom and compassion.
Jesus, for you and your people hospitality was a sacred duty;
    —help us to transform our world into a place that is safe
        for mutual aid and neighborliness.
You were content to let weeds grow among wheat until harvest
time;

—give us the patience to live with our own shortcomings
and those of others.
Our days are often filled with interruptions;
—teach us how to reap the good fruit of patience from
these times.

PRAYER: God our Creator, you have called us by name; we
belong to you. Help us to believe in your truth, hope in
your mercy, and love all people as you call us to love.
Let our lives give joy to you and encouragement to one
another. May our efforts to live in love give you praise
this night and every day of our lives through all
eternity. Amen.

TUESDAY
MORNING PRAYER

**Ant. 1 O God, forgive the sins of
your people.**
Psalm 85

O God, once you favored your
land,
restoring the fortunes of Rachel
and Jacob.
You forgave the guilt of your
people;
you pardoned all their sins.
You withdrew your wrath;
you calmed the heat of your anger.

Restore us again,
O God our salvation,
put away your grievance against
us!
Will you be angry with us forever,
Will you prolong it to all
generations?

Will you not restore us again,
that your people may rejoice in
you?
Show us your steadfast love,
and grant us your salvation.

Let me hear what you have to say,
for you will speak peace to your
people,
to those who are near you,
and who turn to you in their
hearts.
Your salvation is near for those
who fear you,
that glory may dwell in our land.

Mercy and truth have embraced;
justice and peace will kiss.
Truth shall spring out of the earth,
and justice will look down from
heaven.

You will give what is good,
our land will yield its increase.
Justice shall go before you
and make a path for your steps.
Glory*...

**Ant. 2 O God, grant peace to all
peoples.**
Cant: Isaiah 26:1b–4, 7–9, 12

A strong city have we, O God;
you set up salvation—

like walls and ramparts.
Open the gates
that the nation which keeps faith
may enter in.

You keep those in perfect peace,
whose minds are fixed on you,
because they trust in you,
trust in you forever.
For you are our God,
an everlasting Rock.

The way of the just is level;
you make smooth the path of the
   just.
In the path of your judgments,
we wait for you;
your name remembered from of
   old,
is the desire of our souls.

My soul yearns for you in the
   night,
my spirit within me keeps vigil;
when your judgments abide in the
   earth,
the inhabitants of the world learn
   justice.

O God, you ordain peace for all
   people,—

you accomplish all our works.
   Glory*...

**Ant. 3 In the light of your face
there is life, O God.**
Psalm 67

O God, be gracious to us and bless
   us
and make your face shine upon
   us.
That your ways be known upon
   earth,
your saving power among all
   nations.
Let the peoples praise you, O God;
let all the peoples praise you.

Let the nations be glad and sing
   for joy,
for you judge the peoples with
   equity
and guide the nations on earth.
Let the peoples praise you, O God;
let all the peoples praise you.

The earth has yielded its increase;
God, our God, has blessed us.
You, indeed, have blessed us;
let all the earth revere you!
   Glory*...

READING

RESPONSORY

It is good to give thanks to you and sing praise to your name.
   —It is good...
At the works of your hands I shout for joy, **—and sing...**
Glory to you, Source of all Being, Eternal Word and Holy Spirit.
   —It is good...

CANTICLE OF ZECHARIAH

**Ant. I will praise you from the rising of the sun to its going
   down.**

INTERCESSIONS

O God, you have blessed humankind with understanding,
imagination and memory;
>—show us how to learn from the past and to plan for the
>future.

The gifts of the earth are distributed unevenly, and we long to lift
up those in need;
>—soften the hearts of those who place personal or national
>gain above the good of the whole.

Jesus, you have gifted us with the revelation of God's love;
>—let your love bear abundant fruit in our lives.

You preached to the crowds, inviting them to sit on grassy
hillsides;
>—open our eyes to the beauty of our world, and make us
>understand the need to protect our environment.

Spirit of God, life-giving presence to every person;
>—make your compassion and love known to those who
>suffer abuse, torture, and sub-human conditions.

PRAYER: Giver of hope, we begin a new day confident that you
come to us in all circumstances and make all things
work for the fulfillment of your purposes. We praise
you for your wonderful works through Christ who has
shown us the way. Amen.

DAYTIME PRAYER

**Ant. 1 I will ponder your law
within my heart.
Psalm 119:97–104**

How I love your law, O God!
It is my meditation all the day.
Your commandment makes me
wiser than the learned,
for it is ever with me.

I have more understanding than
all my teachers,
for your will is my meditation.
I have more understanding than
the aged,
for I keep your precepts.

I turn my feet from evil ways,
to obey your word.
I turn not aside from your decrees,
for you, yourself, have taught me.

How sweet are your words to my
taste,
sweeter than honey to my mouth!
Through your precepts I gain
understanding;
therefore I hate every false way.
Glory*...

Ant. 2 Restore your dwelling place within us.
Psalm 74

Why have you cast us off forever?
Why blaze with anger against the
  sheep of your pasture?
Remember your people whom you
  chose from of old,
which you redeemed as your
  heritage!
Remember Mount Zion where you
  made your dwelling.

Direct your steps to the eternal
  ruins,
everything destroyed in your
  sanctuary!
Evil has roared in your house of
  prayer,
setting up its signs for symbols.

At the upper entrance they hacked
the wooden trellis with axes.
With hatchets and hammers,
broke down its carved wood.
The sanctuary they set on fire,
desecrating the place where you
  dwell.

They said to themselves, "We will
  utterly crush them;"
and burned all the shrines in the
  land.
We do not see our signs any more;
there is no longer a prophet,
no one knows how long it will last.

How long, O God, is evil to
  conquer?
Is your name to be scoffed forever?
Why do you hold back your hand,
Why do you keep your hand
  concealed?

Yet you are our ruler from of old,
working salvation in the midst of
  the earth.   **Glory*...**

Ant. 3 Yours is the day, yours is the night; all things are in your hands.

II

It was you who divided the sea by
  your might,
who shattered the heads of the
  monsters in the sea.

You crushed the heads of
  Leviathan,
and gave them as food to the
  creatures of the wilderness.
You split open springs and brooks;
dried up the ever-flowing streams.

Yours is the day and yours is the
  night;
you fixed the stars and the sun.
You established all the bounds of
  earth;
you made both summer and
  winter.

Remember then, how evil scoffs,
and how your name is reviled.
Do not deliver your dove to the
  hawk:
do not forget the lives of your poor.

Remember your covenant of old;
for violence dwells in every corner
  of the land.
Let not the downtrodden be put to
  shame;
let the poor and the needy bless
  your name.

Arise, O God, defend your cause!
Remember how you are reviled all
  the day.—

Quiet those who clamor against you,—

who clamor against you day after day. **Glory*...**

PRAYER: God of love, you gave us this universe filled with your gifts. Help us to reverence all of your creation, respecting the rights of all species, and the integrity of the elements. Teach us to realize in our hearts as well as in our minds that we praise you when we use your gifts as you meant them to be used. May we unite with all suffering creation in the struggle for liberation from all that seeks to destroy. Grant this that all creation may live with you for all eternity. Amen.

EVENING PRAYER

Ant. 1 You are round about your people, both now and forever.

Psalm 125

Those who put their trust in you
are like Mount Zion;
it cannot be moved, but stands
forever.

As the mountains are round about
Jerusalem,
so are you round about your
people,
both now and forever.

For the scepter of wickedness
shall not rest
over the land of the just,
lest the just put forth their hands
to turn to evil ways.

Do good, O God, to those who are
good,
to those who are upright of heart!
But those who turn to evil ways,
will be chastised and punished!

On Israel, peace! **Glory*...**

Ant. 2 Blessed are those who are pure of heart.

Psalm 131

O God, my heart is not lifted up,
my eyes are not raised too high;
I have not occupied myself
with marvels beyond me.

I have calmed and quieted my
soul,
like a child at its mother's breast;
like a child in its father's arms,
even so my soul.

O Israel, hope in your God
both now and forever.
Glory*....

Ant. 3 Let all creation serve you, for you created all things.
Cant: Rev 4:11, 5:9, 10, 12

Worthy are you, O God, our God,
to receive glory and honor and
power.

For you have created all things;
by your will they came to be and
were made.

Worthy are you to take the scroll
and to open its seals,

For you were slain, and by your
blood,
you purchased for God
saints of every race and tongue,
of every people and nation.

You have made of them a kindom,-

and priests to serve our God,
and they shall reign on the earth.

Worthy is the Lamb who was slain
to receive power and riches,
wisdom and strength,
honor and glory and praise.
          Glory*...

READING

RESPONSORY

Teach us to number our days that we may gain wisdom
      of heart.—**Teach us...**
Let your works be manifest to your servants; —**that we...**
Glory to you, Source of all Being, Eternal Word and Holy Spirit.
      —**Teach us...**

CANTICLE OF MARY

Ant. You who are mighty have done great things for me.

INTERCESSIONS

O God, the wonders of communication have made our world
smaller but more complex;
      —bless the United Nations with wise and magnanimous
         leaders.
Jesus, you teach us of the realm of God with wonderful and
effective images;
      —inspire teachers and writers with the creativity they need
         to expand our minds and hearts.
Ask, knock, seek is your invitation to us to take our needs to God;
      —make us quick to respond to the needs of those who ask;
         make us aware of those so needy they cannot ask.
Spirit of God, you take flesh in us and for us;
      —keep us open to all who inspire us to grow; prophets,
         athletes, philosophers, artists, and all who serve us in
         your name.
Time is your gift to us, O God; let us not take it for granted;
      —show us efficient ways to use and share it.

PRAYER: O God, you are both mother and father to us. Help us to reverence all people with whom we share such great love, and show us the way to peace in our world. We ask this as your children through Jesus, our brother. Amen.

WEDNESDAY

MORNING PRAYER

Ant 1 Gladden my soul, O God; for to you I lift up my heart.

Psalm 86

Incline your ear and give answer,
for I am poor and needy.
Preserve my life, for I am faithful:
save the servant who trusts in you.

You are my God, have mercy on me,
for to you I cry all the day.
Gladden the soul of your servant,
for to you I lift up my soul.

O God, you are good and forgiving,
abounding in love to all who call.
Give ear to my prayer;
hearken to my supplication.
In the day of my trouble I call on you,
for you will answer me.

There is none like you among the gods,
nor works to compare with yours.
All the nations you made
shall come and bow down,
shall glorify your name.
For you are great and do wondrous things,
you alone are God.

Teach me your way, O God,
that I may walk in your truth;—

cause my heart to fear your name.
I give thanks to you with all my heart,
and glorify your name forever.
For great toward me is your love;
you deliver my soul from the grave.

Pride has risen against me;
corruption pursues my life,
evil pays you no heed.
But you are merciful and gracious,
slow to anger, abounding in love.

Turn to me and take pity;
give strength to your servant,
and save your handmaid's child.
Show me a sign of your favor;
let injustice be put to shame,
help me and give me your comfort. **Glory*...**

Ant. 2 Blessed are the just, who speak the truth.
Cant: Isaiah 33:13–16

Hear, you who are far off,
what I have done;
you who are near,
acknowledge my might.

The sinners in Zion are afraid;
trembling grips the impious;
"Who of us can live with the devouring fire?—

Who of us can live with the
everlasting flames?"

Those who walk justly and speak
honestly,
who spurn what is gained by
oppression,
who shake their hands,
free of contact with a bribe;
who stop their ears,
lest they hear of bloodshed,
who close their eyes,
lest they look on evil.

They shall dwell on the heights;
their place of refuge
shall be the rocky fortress;
their food will be given,
their water will be sure.
   Glory*...

**Ant. 3 Let us sing a joyful song
in the presence of our God.
Psalm 98**

We sing to you a new song,
for you have done wonderful
things!
Your saving hand and your holy
arm
have given the victory.

You have made known your
salvation;
have revealed your justice to the
nations.
You have remembered your love
and your faithfulness
for the house of Israel.
All the ends of the earth have
seen
the salvation of our God.

Make a joyful noise, all the earth;
break forth into joyous song!
Sing praise to God with the harp,
with the lyre and the sound of
music!
With trumpets and the sound of
the horn
make a joyful noise to our God.

Let the sea roar and all that fills
it;
the world and those who dwell in
it!
Let the rivers clap their hands;
and the hills ring out their joy.

All creation sings before God
who comes to judge the earth.
God will judge the world with
justice
and the peoples with equity.
   Glory.

READING

RESPONSORY

Satisfy us in the morning with your steadfast love, that we may
   rejoice and be glad all our days. —**Satisfy us...**
Let the favor of God be upon us; —**that we...**
Glory to you, Source of all Being, Eternal Word and Holy Spirit.
   —**Satisfy us...**

CANTICLE OF ZECHARIAH

Ant. Remember the mercy you promised long ago.

INTERCESSIONS

Jesus, you preached a kindom not of this world, but you were ever mindful to provide food for your followers;
>—grant success to those who draw food from our waters and fields; keep them safe and their methods environmentally sound.

You blessed little children and warned us against misleading them;
>—give wisdom to those who become parents while they are still children themselves.

O God, you call us all to unity through Jesus;
>—show yourself to those who are estranged from one another, and bridge their differences with the fire of your love.

Jesus, you frowned upon the ambitions of your apostles;
>—let our ambition and goal be to offer you a life of love and dedicated service as we care for one another.

Bless the ministers of your church;
>—guide them to serve as you have served.

PRAYER: God of unity and peace, may the gift of your life within us show itself in concrete ways so that we may make clear with our lives the good news of Jesus Christ. Especially today we pray for all the children of this world, that they may know your love and the hope of peace on earth. Grant this prayer that all may know the gift you gave in Jesus. Amen.

DAYTIME PRAYER

Ant. 1 Your Word is the true light that enlightens all who come into the world.

Psalm 119:105–112

O God, your word is a lamp to my feet
and a light for my path.
I have sworn an oath and confirmed it,
to observe your commandments.

I am sorely afflicted:
give me life according to your word!
Accept my offerings of praise,
and teach me your decrees.

Though I hold my life in my hands,
I do not forget your law.
Though the wicked try to ensnare me,
I do not stray from your precepts.

Your will is my heritage forever,
the joy of my heart.
I incline my heart to carry out
  your will forever, to endless
  ages. **Glory*...**

**Ant. 2 Hear my prayer and
  hasten to help me.**
Psalm 70

Be pleased, O God, to save me!
O God, make haste to help me!
Fill me with shame and confusion
if I turn away from life!

O let me turn back in confusion,
when I delight in wrongdoing!
Let me retreat in my shame,
when I trifle with evil.

May all who seek you
rejoice and be glad!
May those who love your
  salvation
proclaim, "Our God is great!"

But I am poor and needy;
hasten to me, O God!
You are my help, my deliverer;
O God, do not delay. **Glory*...**

**Ant. 3 You know the hearts of
  all; your judgment is right and
  true.**
Psalm 75

We give thanks to you, O God;—

we give you thanks;
we call on your name
and recount your wondrous
  deeds.

"At the time which I appoint
I will judge with equity.
When the earth totters,
and all its inhabitants,
it is I who steady its pillars.

To the boastful I say: 'Do not
  boast,'
to the wicked, 'Do not flaunt your
  strength,
do not flaunt your strength on
  high,
or speak with insolent pride.'"

For not from the east or from the
  west,
or from the wilderness comes
  judgment,
but you, O God, are the judge,
putting down one, lifting up
  another.

But I will rejoice forever,
I will sing praises to you on high.
You shall break the power of
  wickedness,
while the strength of the just
  shall be exalted. **Glory*...**

PRAYER: O God, you both comfort us and disturb our
  complacency through your Spirit. May we recognize
  the blind, the lame, and the prisoner in the
  circumstances of our lives, and understand our
  call to proclaim the good news to the poor. We
  ask this through Jesus who is our way, our truth,
  and our life. Amen.

EVENING PRAYER

Ant. 1 You will not reject me; you will fill my mouth with laughter.
Psalm 126

When God restored the fortunes of Zion,
it seemed like a dream.
Then our mouth was filled with laughter,
and our tongue with shouts of joy;

Then they said among the nations,
"God has done great things for them."
You have done great things for us!
Indeed we are glad.

Restore our fortunes, O God,
like the streams in the desert!
May those who sow in tears
reap with shouts of joy!

They that go forth weeping,
bearing seed for the sowing,
shall come home with shouts of joy,
bringing their sheaves with them.
Glory*...

Ant. 2 Wisdom has built herself a house!
Psalm 127

If God does not build the house,
its builders labor in vain.
If God does not watch over the city,
in vain is the vigil kept.

It is vain to rise up early
and go late to rest,
eating the bread of anxious toil:—
for you, O God, give sleep to your beloved.

Truly children are a gift from the Most High,
the fruit of the womb, a blessing.
Like arrows in the hand of a warrior
are the children of one's youth.

Happy the couple who have their quiver full of them!
They shall not be put to shame
when they encounter distress.
Glory*...

Ant. 3 Jesus is the image of the invisible God.
Cant: Colossians 1:12–20

Let us give thanks to God
for having made us worthy
to share the inheritance of the saints in light.

God has delivered us
from the power of darkness
and transferred us
into the kindom of God's beloved Son, Jesus,
in whom we have redemption,
the forgiveness of our sins.

Jesus is the image of the invisible God,
the first-born of all creation;
in him all things were created,
in heaven and on earth,
things visible and invisible.

All things were created through him;
all were created for him.
He is before all else that is.
In him all things hold together.

He is the head of the body, the church!
He is the beginning,
the firstborn from the dead,
that in everything, he might be above all others.

In him all the fullness of God was pleased to dwell,
and, through him, to reconcile all things to himself,
whether on earth or in heaven,
making peace by the blood of his cross. **Glory*...**

READING

RESPONSORY

You will cover us with your pinions, and under your wings we will find refuge. **—You will...**
We will not fear the terror of the night; **—and under...**
Glory to you, Source of all Being, Eternal Word and Holy Spirit. **—You will...**

CANTICLE OF MARY

Ant. Holy is the name of our God.

INTERCESSIONS

Jesus, you knew a laborer's day;
   —bless those who live by the work of their hands; help all to find the employment they need.
The world still longs for the peace that only you can give;
   —guard and protect those whose work is to keep the peace in lands torn by war and revolution.
In your kindom the last shall be first and the first last;
   —encourage and liberate minorities, those whose lot is mostly last.
Enlighten and encourage those committed to you in religious vocations;
   —let their lives reflect their calling.
Have mercy on all who are touched by the drug epidemic in our world;
   —lead them to freedom through the good news enfleshed in those who reach out to them.

PRAYER: Jesus, light of the world, for the many who have followed you today through the darkness of temptation, doubt, or pain, you are the promise of an eternal dawn. We give thanks for all that has been given to us through you, and we ask for the grace to be your faithful disciples. May we praise you all the days of our lives. Amen.

THURSDAY

MORNING PRAYER

Ant. 1 Blessed are those who delight in your law, O God.
Psalm 1

Blessed are those who walk not in
 the counsel of the wicked,
nor stand in the way of sinners,
nor sit with those who scoff;
but delight in your law, O God,
pondering it day and night.

They are like a tree
planted by streams of water,
that yields its fruit in due season,
and whose leaves never fade.
May they prosper in all they do.

It is not so with wickedness.
Like chaff the wind drives it away.
Evil cannot stand before you,
nor injustice before your face.

For you guide the path of the
 faithful,
but renounce the way of
 oppression. **Glory*...**

Ant. 2 God will come with justice for all the people.
Cant: Isaiah 40:10–17

Behold, you come with power,
O God, the Almighty,
ruling with your strong arm;
behold, your reward is with you,
and your recompense before you.

You will feed your flock like a
 shepherd,
you will gather the lambs in your
 arms,
carrying them in your bosom,
gently leading the ewes with
 young.

Who else had measured the waters
in the hollows of their hands,
and marked off the heavens with a
 span,
enclosed the dust of the earth in a
 measure,
weighed the mountains in scales
and the hills in a balance?

Who has directed your spirit,
or who has been your counselor?
Whom did you consult for
 enlightenment,
who taught you the path of justice,
or showed you the way of
 understanding?

Behold, the nations are like a drop
 from a bucket,
accounted as dust on the scales;
you take up the isles like powder.

Lebanon would not suffice for fuel,
nor its beasts be enough for burnt
 offering.
All the nations are as nothing
 before you,
as nothing and void are they
 accounted. **Glory*...**

Ant. 3 We worship and give praise to you, Most High.
Psalm 99

O God, you reign on high;
let all the peoples tremble!
You are throned on the cherubim;
let the earth quake!
You are great in Zion.

You are exalted over all peoples.
Let them praise your name,
    awesome and great!
Holy are you over all!

Mighty Sovereign, lover of justice,
you have established equity;
you have ruled with justice.
We extol you, Most High God;
worshipping at your footstool!
You alone are holy.

Moses and Aaron were among
    your priests,
among your petitioners, Judith
    and Esther.
They invoked you, and you
    answered.
You spoke to them in the pillar of
    cloud;
they kept your will,
and the precepts that you gave
    them.

O God, our God, you answered
    them;
you were a forgiving God to them,
yet you punished their offenses.

We extol you, Most High God,
and worship on your holy
    mountain;
for you alone are holy.
        Glory*...

READING

RESPONSORY

No one who practices deceit shall dwell in your house.
    —No one...
They who walk in the way that is blameless **—shall dwell...**
Glory to you, Source of all Being, Eternal Word and Holy Spirit.
    —No one...

CANTICLE OF ZECHARIAH

Ant. Guide our feet, O God, into the way of peace.

INTERCESSIONS

O God, we praise you for the gift of faith and for all that our
baptism means to us;
    —help us to keep our commitment to you alive and active
        and to cherish and remember special moments of insight.
You answer our prayers and fulfill our needs;
    —make us aware of the needs of others and generous in
        ministering to them.

Jesus, you were called the carpenter's son, an attempt to
discredit you;
> —give us the grace we need to see one another in truth, to
> hold each other's heritage with reverence, and to realize
> that we are one in you.

Your disciples left all to follow you;
> —be praised in the missionaries who leave all that is
> familiar to them to give your message to the world.

You are resurrection and life to all who hope in you;
> —give courage and peace to those who await your coming.

PRAYER: O God, we are the work of your hands, and you have
made us for communion with you and one another. As
we begin the business of this day, we recall that you
alone can fill our hearts. We ask to remain by love in
your holy presence, with Jesus, who incarnated your
presence among us. Amen.

DAYTIME PRAYER

**Ant. 1 Sustain me, O God,
according to your promise.
Psalm 119:113–120**

I have no love for the half-hearted,
but I love your law.
You are my shelter, my shield;
I hope in your word.

Rid me of all that is evil,
that I may keep your
commandments.
Uphold me according to your
promise,
that I may live in your way,
let my hopes not be in vain!

Sustain me and I shall be safe
and ever observe your statutes.
Help me spurn all that is evil;
let its cunning be in vain!

You overthrow all that is wicked;
therefore I love your will.
I tremble before you in awe,—

I am afraid of your judgments.
Glory*...

**Ant. 2 Rescue us, O God, for the
sake of your name.
Psalm 79:1–5, 8–11, 13**

O God, the nations have invaded
our land,
they have defiled your holy temple;
Jerusalem is in ruins.
They have given the bodies of your
servants
as food to the birds of the air,
and the flesh of your faithful
to the beasts of the earth.

They have poured out blood like
water round about Jerusalem,
no one is left to bury the dead.
We have become the taunt of our
neighbors,
mocked and derided by those
round about us.

How long, O God? Will you be
  angry forever,
how long will your anger burn like
  fire?
Do not hold against us the guilt of
  our ancestors;
Let your compassion hasten to
  meet us;
for we are brought very low.

Help us, O God, our savior,
for the glory of your name;
deliver us, and forgive us our sins,
rescue us for the sake of your
  name.

Why should the nations say,
"Where is their God?"
Let us see oppression overthrown,
may justice come to Jerusalem!
Let the groans of the prisoners
  come before you;
let your strong arm preserve those
  condemned to die!

Then we your people, the flock of
  your pasture,
will give you thanks for ever;
from generation to generation
we will recount your praise.
  Glory*...

**Ant. 3 O God, you are the
vinedresser; prune the vine
that it may bear fruit.**

Psalm 80

Give ear, O Shepherd of Israel,
you who lead Joseph like a flock!
You who are enthroned upon the
  cherubim,
shine forth before Ephraim,
  Benjamin and Manasseh!
Stir up your might and come to
  save us!

Restore us, God of hosts;
let your face shine, that we may be
  saved.
God of hosts, how long will you be
  angry
with your people's prayers?
You fed them with the bread of
  tears,
and gave them tears to drink in
  full measure.
You made us the scorn of our
  neighbors,
our enemies laugh among
  themselves.

Restore us, God of hosts;
let your face shine, that we may be
  saved.

You brought a vine out of Egypt;
you drove out the nations to plant
  it.
You cleared the ground before it;
it took root and filled the land.

The mountains were covered with
  its shade,
the mighty cedars with its
  branches;
it sent out its branches to the sea,
and its roots to the Great River.

Then why have you broken down
  its walls?
so that all who pass by pluck its
  fruit?
It is ravaged by the boar of the
  forest,
devoured by the beasts of the field.

Turn again, O God of hosts!
Look down from heaven, and see;
have regard for this vine,
the vine your own hand has
  planted.
It has been burnt with fire and cut
  down.

Let your hand be on those you
have chosen,
those you make strong for
yourself!
Then we will never forsake you;—

give us life, and we will call on
your name.

Restore us, God of hosts!
let your face shine, that we may be
saved. **Glory*...**

PRAYER: Renew in our hearts, O God, the gift of your Holy
Spirit, so that we may love you fully in all that we do
and love one another as Christ loves us. May all that
we do proclaim the good news that you are God with
us. Amen.

EVENING PRAYER

**Ant. 1 Let us enter your courts
with shouts of praise.**

Psalm 132

O God, remember David,
all the many hardships he
endured;
the oath he swore to you,
his vow to the Strong One of
Jacob.

"I will not enter my house or get
into my bed;
I will give no sleep to my eyes,
or slumber to my eyelids,
till I find a place for my God,
a dwelling for the Strong One of
Jacob."

We heard of it in Ephrathah,
we found the ark in the fields of
Jaar.
"Let us go to the place of God's
dwelling;
let us worship at God's footstool."

Go up, O God, to the place of your
rest,
you and the ark of your might.
Let your priests be clothed with
justice,
and your faithful shout for joy.—

For the sake of David your servant
do not reject your anointed.
Glory*...

**Ant. 2 You, O God, have chosen
Zion as your dwelling place.**
II

You swore an oath to David;
from which you will not turn back:
"A son, the fruit of your body,
I will set upon your throne.

If your offspring keep my covenant
in truth,
and my laws which I shall teach
them,
their descendants also forever
shall sit upon your throne."

For you have chosen Zion;
you desired it for your dwelling:
"This is my resting place forever;
here I have desired to dwell.

I will abundantly bless its
provisions;
I will satisfy its poor with bread.
I will clothe its priests with
salvation,
and its faithful will shout for joy.

There David's stock will flower:—

I will prepare a lamp for my
   anointed.
Treacherous plots will be put to
   shame,
but on him my crown shall shine."
   Glory*...

**Ant. 3 The glory of God is the
   light of the city, and its lamp
   is the Lamb.**
         **Cant: Rev 11:17–18;
               12:10b–12a**

We praise you, God Almighty,
who is and who was.
You have assumed your great
   power,
you have begun your reign.

The nations have raged in anger,
but then came your day of wrath
and the moment to judge the
   dead;—

the time to reward your servants
   the prophets
and the holy ones who revere you,
the great and the small alike.

Now have salvation and power
   come,
your reign, O God, and the
   authority of your Anointed One.
For the accusers of our loved ones
   have been cast out,
who night and day accused them.

By the blood of the Lamb have
   they been defeated,
and by the testimony of your
   servants;
love for life did not deter them
   from death.
So rejoice, you heavens,
and you that dwell therein!
   Glory*...

READING

RESPONSORY

How great are your works, O God. Your thoughts are very deep.
   —How great...
The dull of heart will never know. **—Your thoughts...**
Glory to you, Source of all Being, Eternal Word and Holy Spirit.
   —How great...

CANTICLE OF MARY

Ant. Your mercy endures through all generations.

INTERCESSIONS

Jesus, you invited Peter to follow you in ways beyond his courage;
   —increase our faith, that we may be ready and willing
      instruments of your love.
You caution us over and over again to stay awake, to be on guard;
   —give us the gift of discernment; help us to live consciously,
      learning from the past as we plan for the future.

O God, bless those whom you call to the single life;
—let their commitment to the gospel be a joy to you,
   enrichment for them, and a service to others that mirrors
   your Christ.
O God, give us a desire for true and lasting values;
—let our faith in you inform all that we are and do.
Spirit of God, you bring both peace and fire to our hearts;
—teach us how to challenge and affirm one another in a
   spirit of harmony.

PRAYER: Most gentle God, you have fed us this day with your
holy Word and life-giving Bread. May we continue to
discern your calls in life, family, community and in the
movements of our hearts. May we always be among
those who worship you in spirit and in truth. We ask
this through the intercession of all those who gave their
lives that others may have bread and a better quality of
life. Amen.

FRIDAY

MORNING PRAYER

**Ant 1 A humble, contrite heart,
O God, you will not despise.**
Psalm 51

Have mercy on me, O God,
according to your steadfast love;
in your abundant mercy blot out
   my sins.
Wash me thoroughly from my
   offenses,
and cleanse me from my sin!

For I know my offenses,
and my sin is ever before me.
Against you, you alone, have I
   sinned,
and done what is evil in your
   sight,
so you are justified in your
   sentence—

and blameless in your judgment.
Behold, I was brought forth in a
   sinful world.

For you desire truth in my
   innermost being;
teach me wisdom in the depths of
   my heart.
O purify me, and I shall be clean;
O wash me, I shall be whiter than
   snow.
Fill me with joy and gladness;
let the bones you have broken
   rejoice.
Hide your face from my guilt,
and blot out all my offenses.

Create in me a clean heart,
put a steadfast spirit within me.
Cast me not from your presence,
take not your spirit from me.—

Give me again the joy of your
    salvation,
with a willing spirit uphold me.

Then I will teach transgressors
    your ways,
and sinners will return to you.
Deliver me from death,
O God of my salvation,
and my tongue will sing out your
    saving help.

Open my lips and my mouth will
    sing your praises.
For you take no delight in
    sacrifice;
were I to give a burnt offering,
you would not be pleased.
A broken spirit you accept;
a contrite heart, you will not
    despise.

In your goodness, show favor to
    Zion;
rebuild the walls of Jerusalem.
Then you will delight in just
    sacrifices,
in gifts offered on your altar.
    Glory*...

**Ant. 2 You bring us to springs
of water; you will wipe away
every tear from our eyes.
Cant: Jeremiah 14:17–21**

Let my eyes stream with tears
night and day, without rest,
for the virgin daughter of my
    people
is smitten with a great wound,
with a very grievous blow.

If I walk out into the field,
behold those slain by the sword!
If I enter the city,
behold the diseases of famine!
Both the prophet and the priest
ply their trade throughout the
    land,—

ignorant of their doings.

Have you utterly rejected Judah?
Is Zion loathsome to you?
Why have you smitten us
so that there is no healing?

We looked for peace to no avail;
for a time of healing,
but terror comes instead.
We acknowledge our wickedness,
and the guilt of our ancestors,
for we have sinned against you.

Spurn us not for your name's
    sake;
do not dishonor your glorious
    throne;
remember your covenant with us,
and break it not.   **Glory*...**

**Ant. 3 We are your people, the
sheep of your pasture.
Psalm 100**

All the earth cries out to you with
    shouts of joy, O God,
Serving you with gladness;
coming before you, singing for
    joy.

You, Creator of all, are God.
You made us, we belong to you,
we are your people, the sheep of
    your pasture.

We enter your gates with
    thanksgiving,
and your courts with songs of
    praise!
We give you thanks and bless
    your name.

Indeed, how good you are,
enduring, your steadfast love.
You are faithful to all generations.
    Glory*...

READING

RESPONSORY

Return, O God! How long? Have pity on your servants. **—Return...**
Satisfy us in the morning with your steadfast love. **—Have...**
Glory to you, Source of all Being, Eternal Word and Holy Spirit.
    —Return...

CANTICLE OF ZECHARIAH

Ant. Give light to those in darkness and the shadow of death.

INTERCESSIONS

O God, a humble heart is more pleasing to you than sacrifice;
    —lift up all who are humiliated and despised because of
        their own faults or those of others.
Faith is your free gift to us, O God;
    —enlighten us with ways of sharing it with others.
O God, your love is eternal, and we fail you "seven times a day";
    —preserve us from measuring you by our own pettiness;
        never let fear keep us from turning to you.
Jesus, you have made yourself as available to us as bread;
    —help us to realize our need to live in your presence and to
        listen to the voice of your spirit in our hearts.
Spirit of God, love is your gift to us and the gift you desire from
us;
    —receive our desire and poor efforts to offer you our lives
        this day.

PRAYER: Direct our activity this day, O merciful God, that we
            may reflect your goodness and love to our companions.
            Help us to be mindful of the many people who are
            oppressed, and may we be aware of the ways that we
            oppress others. We ask this in the name of Jesus who
            died to set us free. Amen.

DAYTIME PRAYER

Ant. 1 The servant of God was stricken; smitten by God, and afflicted.

Psalm 22

O God, my God, why have you forsaken me?
Why are you so far from helping me,
from the sound of my groaning?
I cry out by day, but you do not answer;
by night, but find no rest.

Yet you alone are holy,
enthroned on the praises of Israel.
In you our ancestors trusted;
they trusted and you delivered them.
To you they cried, and were saved;
In you they trusted,
and were not disappointed.

But I am a worm and not human,
scorned and despised by the people.
All who see me mock at me,
they curl their lips, they wag their heads;
"You trusted in God, let God save you;
let God rescue you,
for God delights in you!"

Yet it was you who took me from the womb;
you kept me safe upon my mother's breasts.
Upon you was I cast from my birth,
since my mother's womb you have been my God.
Be not far from me in my distress;—

there is no one else to help.
Glory*...

Ant. 2 By oppression and judgment, the just one was cut off from the land of the living.

II

Many bulls encompass me,
strong bulls of Bashan surround me;
they open wide their mouths,
like a ravening and roaring lion.

I am poured out like water,
disjointed are all my bones;
my heart has become like wax,
melted within my breast;
my strength is dried up like burnt clay,
my tongue cleaves to my jaws;
you lay me in the dust of death.

Many dogs are round about me;
a band of evildoers encircles me;
they pierce my hands and my feet;
I can count every one of my bones.
They stare and gloat over me;
they divide my garments among them,
for my raiment they cast lots.

But you, O God, be not far off!
O my help, hasten to my aid!
Deliver my soul from the sword,
my life from the grip of the dog!
Save me from the jaws of the lion,
my poor soul from the horns of the wild ox!

I will tell of your name to my kinsfolk
and praise you in the assembly.
Glory*...

Ant. 3 For a moment I hid my face, but I will have compassion on you.

III

You who fear God, give praise!
You descendants of Jacob, give glory!
Stand in awe, children of Israel!

For you, O God, have not despised
nor scorned the affliction of the poor;
you have not hid your face from them,
but heard them when they cried to you.

To you comes praise from the great assembly;
my vows I will pay before those who fear you.
The poor shall eat and be satisfied;—

those who seek you shall sing your praise!
May their hearts live forever and ever!

All the earth shall remember
and turn to you, O God;
all families of the nations
shall worship before you.
For sovereignty belongs to you;
you rule over the nations.

All the mighty of the earth
bow down before you;
before you shall bow
all who go down to the dust.

Posterity shall serve you;
They shall tell of you
to generations yet to come,
and proclaim your deliverance
to a people yet unborn:
"These things our God has done."
Glory*...

PRAYER: Look upon us, most gracious God, as we gather at midday. Bless the work of our hands and hearts. May all peoples be blessed with the dignity of work, with an understanding of their gifts and with generous spirits, so that together we may further your reign among us. Help all who are unemployed and those who are disabled. May all know their worth and dignity. Grant this is Jesus' name. Amen.

EVENING PRAYER

Ant. 1 Our God is high above all other gods.

Psalm 135

We praise your name, O God,
all your servants give praise,
those who stand in your holy house,
in the courts of your house, O God!

We praise you, for you are good.
Sing to your name for you are gracious!
For you have chosen Jacob for yourself,
Israel as your own possession.

For I know that you are great,
that you are high above all gods.
You do whatever you please,—

in heaven and on earth,
in the seas and all the deeps.

You summon clouds from the end
of the earth,
make lightning for the rain,
and bring forth wind from your
storehouse.

You smote the firstborn of Egypt,
both of human and beast alike.
Signs and wonders you worked
in the midst of the land of Egypt,
against Pharaoh and all his
servants.

You smote many nations
and slew mighty rulers,
Sihon, king of the Amorites,
Og, the king of Bashan,
and all the kingdoms of Canaan.
You gave their land as a heritage,
a heritage to your people.
Glory*...

**Ant. 2 You are the living God
come down from heaven.**
II

O God, your name endures
forever,
your renown throughout all ages.
You will work justice for your
people,
and have compassion on your
servants.

The idols of the nations are silver
and gold,
the work of human hands.
They have eyes, but they cannot
see;—

they have ears, but they cannot
hear;
nor is there any breath on their
lips.
Like them be those who make
them!
And everyone who trusts in them!

Descendants of Israel, bless our
God!
Descendants of Aaron, bless our
God!
Descendants of Levi, bless our
God!
You who fear, bless the Most
High!

Blessed are you from Zion, O
God,
you who dwell in Jerusalem!
Glory*...

**Ant. 3 Behold I make all things
new!**
Cant: Rev 15:3–4

Great and wonderful are your
works,
God the Almighty One!
Just and true are your ways,
Ruler of all the ages!

Who shall refuse you honor,
or the glory due your name?

For you alone are holy,
all nations shall come and
worship in your presence.
Your judgments are clearly seen.
Glory*...

READING

RESPONSORY

When the cares of my heart are many, your consolations cheer
my soul. —**When the...**

You have become my stronghold; —your...
Glory to you, Source of all Being, Eternal Word and Holy Spirit.
   —When the...

CANTICLE OF MARY

Ant. Fill the hungry with bread of earth and bread of heaven.

INTERCESSIONS

You are our Creator, O God, and you know of what we are made;
   —have mercy on those who are forced to work beyond their
      strength or to bear their limit of suffering.
We thank and praise you for the talents you have given to those
who make our lives less burdensome by invention and more
delightful through art;
   —give them the grace to live balanced and holy lives.
The future is always a mystery to us; our lives are in your hands;
   —grant us a childlike peace as we place our trust in you
      and do our best to serve you.
Jesus, you prayed for unity on the night before you died for us;
   —heal us of our prejudices, and grant success to our efforts
      toward ecumenism.
You radiated the joy that is the sign of the Spirit;
   —let our joy and good humor reveal your presence in our
      lives.

PRAYER: Most loving God, at evening's end we pray for all who
near the evening of their lives. Grant them your peace
and reconciliation with all who love them. May they
know the hope and joy that awaits them when they see
you face to face. This we ask through the intercession
of Joseph and of all who died in your embrace. Amen.

SATURDAY

MORNING PRAYER

**Ant. 1 You are near at hand, O
God, and all your ways are true.
Psalm 119: 145–152**

With all my heart, I cry to you;
answer me, O God.—

I cry to you; save me,
that I may observe your will.

I rise before dawn and cry for help;
I hope in your words.
My eyes watch throughout the
   night—

meditating on your promises.

Hear my voice in your steadfast
  love;
in your justice preserve my life.
Those who persecute me draw
  near;
they are far from your law.

But you, O God, are near at hand,
all your commands are true.
Long have I known that your will
  endures forever.
    Glory*...

**Ant. 2 Give us your Spirit of
Wisdom in all our affairs.**

Cant: Wisdom 9:1–6, 9–11

God of our ancestors, God of
  mercy,
you who have made all things by
  your word
and in your wisdom have
  established us
to care for the creatures produced
  by you,
to govern the world in holiness
  and justice,
and to render judgment in
  integrity of heart.

Give us Wisdom, the attendant at
  your throne,
and reject us not from among your
  children;
for we are your servants; weak and
  short-lived
and lacking in comprehension of
  judgment and of laws.—

Indeed, though some be perfect
  among all the peoples of this
  earth,
if Wisdom, who comes from you,
  be not with them,
they shall be held in no esteem.

Now with you is Wisdom, who
  knows your works
and was present when you made
  the world;
who understands what is pleasing
  in your eyes
and what is conformable with your
  commands.

Send her forth from your holy
  heavens,
and from your glorious throne
  dispatch her,
that she may be with us and work
  with us,
that we may know what is your
  pleasure.

For she knows and understands
  all things,
and will guide us discreetly in our
  affairs
and safeguard us by her glory.
    Glory*....

**Ant. 3 O God, your faithfulness
endures forever.**
        Psalm 117

Praise our God, all you nations!
Acclaim the Most High, all you
  peoples!

For great is your love for us;
and your faithfulness endures
  forever. **Glory*...**

READING

RESPONSORY

I will give heed to the way that is blameless. When will you
    come to me? —**I will...**
I will walk with integrity of heart within my house. —**When...**
Glory to you, Source of all Being, Eternal Word and Holy Spirit.
    —**I will...**

CANTICLE OF ZECHARIAH

Ant. May we serve you in holiness all the days of our lives.

INTERCESSIONS

Jesus, you taught your followers the deepest lessons of life;
    —show us how to teach our children your ways of forgiveness,
        reverence for one another, and mutual support.
To all who would listen, you revealed God as a tender mother
and an understanding father;
    —teach us how to develop and balance the feminine and
        masculine aspects of our lives.
O God, our desires are boundless, but we are limited on every
side;
    —let the discipline of reality be a spur to our creativity.
Bless all children; let their school years be maturing and fruitful
ones for them;
    —inspire our teachers with ways to draw out the best in all.
You left your mother to follow the call of the Spirit;
    —be with those who must leave their families to find work
        in other countries.

PRAYER: You are a God of Wonder, Most Holy One, as you call
    us into being and set us free in your loving plan. Help
    us to grow in understanding the meaning of our
    freedom, so that we may discern wisely and respect
    the gift of freedom in all our sisters and brothers.
    Grant this through the intercession of all who have
    died that others may be free. Amen.

DAYTIME PRAYER

Ant. 1 Deal with us according to the greatness of your love.

Psalm 119:121-128

I have done what is right and
just:
let me not be oppressed.
Guarantee the goodness of your
servant;
let not the proud oppress me.

My eyes grow weak watching for
salvation,
and the fulfillment of your
promise.
Treat your servant according to
the greatness of your love,
and teach me your statutes.

I am your servant; give me
knowledge,
that I may know your will!
It is time for you to act, O God,
for your law has been broken.

Therefore I love your
commandments
more than finest gold.
I guide my steps by your
precepts:
I hate the ways of falsehood.
Glory*...

Ant. 2 Happy are those who take refuge in you.
Psalm 34

I will bless you, O God, at all
times,
your praise always on my lips.
My soul makes its boast in you;
the afflicted shall hear and be
glad.
Glorify our God with me.—

Together let us praise God's
name.

I sought you, and you answered
me;
and delivered me from all my
fears.
Look towards the Most High, and
be radiant;
let your faces not be ashamed.
These poor ones cried; you heard
them,
and saved them from all their
troubles.

Your angel, O God, is encamped
around those who revere you, to
deliver them.
Taste and see that God is good!
Happy are they who take refuge
in you.

Revere the Most High, all you
saints.
Those who revere you, have no
want!
Young lions suffer want and
hunger;
but those who seek you lack no
blessing. **Glory*...**

Ant. 3 Deliver the brokenhearted from all their troubles.

II

Come children, listen to me,
I will teach you to reverence the
Most High.
Who among you longs for life
and many days to enjoy
prosperity?

Keep your tongue from evil,
your lips from speaking deceit.—

Turn aside from evil and do good;
seek peace and pursue it.

God's eyes are turned to the
  righteous,
God's ears toward their cry.
God's face turns away from evil,
that it not be remembered on
  earth.

When the just cry, the Most High
  hears,
and delivers them from their
  troubles.
God is close to the
  brokenhearted;
saving those whose spirits are
  crushed.

Many are the afflictions of the
  just;
they will be delivered from them
  all.
God will keep guard over all their
  bones,
not one of them shall be broken.

Evil shall be its own destruction;
oppression shall be condemned.
You redeem the lives of your
  servants;
those who take refuge in you
  shall not be condemned.
  Glory*...

PRAYER: You gather us together in faith, O God, as a loving
mother and a gentle father. Help us to remember that
your dwelling place is built upon love and peace, and
that to bring about your reign on earth we must follow
your way of peace. We pray for all governments and
legislatures, that they may be mindful of the rights of
all peoples of this world to live in peace and dignity.
Grant this is the name of Jesus. Amen.

WEEK IV

SUNDAY, EVENING PRAYER I

Ant 1 Peace be within you!
Psalm 122

I was glad when they said to me:
"Let us go to the house of God!"
And now our feet are standing
within your gates, O Jerusalem!

Jerusalem, built as a city
bound firmly together,
to which the tribes go up,
the tribes of our God,
as was decreed for Israel,
to give thanks to your holy name.
There thrones for judgment were
  set,
the thrones of the house of David.

Pray for the peace of Jerusalem!
"Peace be to your homes!
Peace be within your walls,
and security within your borders!

For love of my family and friends
I will say: "Peace be within you!"
For the sake of the house of our
  God,
I seek your good. **Glory*...**

Ant 2 From sunrise to sunset,
my soul waits for you.

Psalm 130

Out of the depths I cry to you,
O God, hear my voice!
Let your ears be attentive
to the voice of my supplication.

*Glory to you, Source of all
Being, Eternal Word and Holy
Spirit,

As it was in the beginning is
now and will be forever. Amen.

If you should mark our iniquities,
O God, who could stand?
But with you is found
  forgiveness:
for this we revere you.

My soul waits for you,
in your word I hope;
my soul waits for you
more than those who watch for
  daybreak.

Let Israel hope in you!
For with you there is love,
and fullness of redemption.
And you will redeem Israel
from all its iniquities.
  Glory*...

Ant 3 Let every knee bow at
the name of Jesus.
Cant: Phil 2:6–11

Though he was in the form of
  God,
Jesus did not count equality with
  God
something to be grasped at.

But emptied himself
taking the form of a slave,
being born in human likeness.

Being found in human estate,
he humbled himself and became
  obedient,
obediently accepting death,
even death on a cross!

Therefore God has highly exalted
  him
and bestowed on him the name
above every other name.

So that at the name of Jesus
every knee should bow,—

in heaven, on the earth,
and under the earth,
and every tongue proclaim—
to the glory of God:
Jesus Christ is Lord! **Glory*...**

READING

RESPONSORY

From daybreak to sunset, we praise your name, O God.
   —From daybreak...
Your glory fills the heavens; **—we praise...**
Glory to you, Source of all Being, Eternal Word and Holy Spirit.
   —From daybreak...

CANTICLE OF MARY

Ant. Blessed are the pure of heart, for they shall see God.

INTERCESSIONS

O God, your invitation to grow is ever before us;
   —free us from the need to control; deepen our trust in your
      desire for our good.
Nothing is impossible for you;
   —let our desires be your own, then grant our requests.
Jesus, you promise to raise up those who have died with you;
   —help us to remember that the suffering of life is not
      meaningless.
Bless those who break under the stress of life;
   —give them understanding and compassionate mentors.
Help the agencies of the world that help others;
   —enable them to find homes and sustenance for all refugees.

PRAYER: All-loving God, you restored your people to eternal life
         by raising Jesus from the dead. Make our faith strong
         and our hope sure. May we never doubt that you will
         fulfill the promises you have made to us and to all the
         peoples of this world. Grant this through the prayers
         of all who without seeing have believed and now enjoy
         the gift of eternal life. Amen.

MORNING PRAYER

**Ant. 1 We praise you for your
steadfast love.**

Psalm 118
I

We give thanks to you, for you are
good,
and your steadfast love endures
forever.

Let the descendants of Israel say:
"Your steadfast love endures
forever."
Let the descendants of Aaron say:
"Your steadfast love endures
forever."
Let those who fear you say:
"Your steadfast love endures
forever."

In my distress, I called to you;
you answered me and set me free.
With you at my side I do not fear.
What can anyone do against me?
You are at my side to help me:
I shall withstand all evildoers.

It is better to take refuge in you,
than to trust in people:
it is better to take refuge in you
than to trust in our leaders.

All wickedness surrounded me;
in your name I crushed it.
It surrounded me, surrounded me
on every side;
in your name I cut it off.
It surrounded me like bees;
it blazed like a fire among thorns.
In your name I crushed it.

I was pushed hard, and was falling
but you came to help me.
You are my strength and my song;
you are my salvation.

O God, you have triumphed;
your reign is exalted.
You have triumphed over all;
I shall not die, I shall live
and recount your wondrous deeds.
You have chastened me sorely,
but have not given me over to
death.

Open to me the gates of justice,
that I may enter and give thanks.
This is your gate, O God;
the just shall enter through it.
I thank you for you have answered
me
you alone are my salvation.

The stone which the builders
rejected
has become the cornerstone.
This is your doing, O God,
it is marvelous in our eyes.
This is the day which you have
made;
let us rejoice and be glad in it.

Save us, we beseech you, O God!
O God, grant us success.
Blessed are those who enter
in your holy name.
For you, O God, are our God,
and you have given us light.

Let us go forward in procession
with branches,
up to your holy altar.
You are my God, I thank you.
You are my God, I praise you.
We give thanks to you for you are
good;
and your steadfast love endures
forever. **Glory*...**

Ant. 2 May all your works bless you, (alleluia).
Cant: Daniel 3:52-57

Blessed are you, God of our ancestors,
praiseworthy and exalted above all forever.

Blessed be your holy and glorious name,
praiseworthy and exalted above all for all ages.

Blessed are you in the temple of your glory,
praiseworthy and exalted above all forever.

Blessed are you on the throne of your kindom,
praiseworthy and exalted above all forever.

Blessed are you who look into the depths
from your throne upon the cherubim,
praiseworthy and exalted above all forever.

Blessed are you in the firmament of heaven,
praiseworthy and glorious forever.

Blessed are you by all your works.
We praise and exalt you above all forever. **Glory*...**

Ant. 3 You are wonderful in all your works, O God.
Psalm 150

We praise you, O God, in your holy sanctuary;
we praise you in your mighty heavens.
We praise you for your powerful deeds;
we praise you according to your greatness.

We praise you with trumpet sound;
We praise you with lute and harp!
We praise you with strings and pipe!

We praise you with sounding cymbals,
We praise you with clashing cymbals!
Let everything that breathes,
give praise to you, O God.
Glory*...

READING

RESPONSORY

We praise your goodness, O God, with songs of thanksgiving.
—**We praise...**
We rejoice in your presence; —**with songs...**
Glory to you, Source of all Being, Eternal Word and Holy Spirit.
—**We praise...**

CANTICLE OF ZECHARIAH

Ant. Give us this day our daily bread.

INTERCESSIONS

O God, the whole world was changed and raised up by the coming of your son;
>—let us never take his life or gospel for granted.

You give us the power to be light or darkness for one another on the way to salvation;
>—show us how to transform the stumbling blocks in our lives to ladders of grace for ourselves and for others.

There are many who do not know you or your Christ;
>—send laborers into your harvest.

Jesus, you ate with sinners and stayed with them;
>—let the Eucharist that we share remind us of your forgiveness and constant presence in our lives.

Spirit of God, lead us to wholesome recreations that delight and nourish us;
>—keep us safe as we play, and let us do so with moderation and gratitude.

PRAYER: O God of the morning, you call us to a new day and to a life of resurrection and union with you. Help us to live this day as a people of hope in a world of chaos. May all who face oppression, terror, abuse, or suffering in any way know that you call us to life and happiness in this world as well as the world to come. We ask this through the intercession of all who lived as people of hope in the midst of despair and now live with you in everlasting peace. Amen.

DAYTIME PRAYER

Ant. 1 You are the bread of life, (alleluia).

Psalm 23

O God, you are my shepherd;
I shall not want.
You make me to lie in green
  pastures.
You lead me to restful waters,
to restore my soul.

You guide me in paths of
  righteousness
for the sake of your name.
Even though I walk through the
  valley of the shadow of death,
I fear no evil;
for you are with me;
your crook and your staff
give me comfort.

You prepare a table before me
in the presence of my foes;
you anoint my head with oil,
my cup overflows.

Surely goodness and mercy shall
follow me
all the days of my life;
and I shall dwell in your holy
house forever and ever.
Glory*...

**Ant. 2 More glorious are you
than the everlasting
mountains, (alleluia).
Psalm 76**

O God, you are known in Judah;
Your abode you established in
Jerusalem,
your dwelling place in Zion.
There you broke the flashing
arrows,
the sword, and the weapons of
war.

Glorious are you, more majestic
than the everlasting mountains.
Warriors were stripped of their
spoil,
sinking into death;
those engaged in war, made
powerless at your word.—

At your rebuke, O God,
the makers of war lay stunned.
Glory*...

**Ant. 3 God arose in judgment to
save the oppressed on earth,
(alleluia).**

II

You, alone, O God, strike terror!
Who can stand before you
when your anger is aroused?
From the heavens you utter
judgment;
the earth feared and was still,
when you rose to establish
judgment
to save the oppressed of the
earth.

Human anger will serve to praise
you;
its residue gird you round.
We make vows to you, and fulfill
them.
Let your faithful bring you gifts;
you, who are worthy of awe,
who cut short the lives of leaders
who strike terror in the rulers of
the earth. **Glory*...**

PRAYER: Creator of all, by the paschal mystery you touch our
lives with the healing power of your love. You have
given us the freedom of the children of God. May all
people know this freedom in their hearts and in their
lives, so that they may celebrate your gift and find joy
in it now and forever. Amen.

EVENING PRAYER II

**Ant. 1 We are a priestly people;
let us give thanks, (alleluia).**
Psalm 110:1-5, 7

God's revelation to the Anointed
  One:
"Sit at my side:
till I put injustice beneath your
  feet."

God will send forth from Zion
your scepter of power:
rule in the midst of your foes.

Your people will give themselves
  freely
on the day you lead your host
upon the holy mountains.
From the womb of the morning
your youth will come like dew.

God has sworn an oath that will
  not be changed.
"You are a priest forever,
after the order of Melchizedek."

The Anointed standing by your
  side,
will shatter rulers on the day of
  wrath.

Drinking from your streams by
  the wayside
shall the Chosen One be
  refreshed. **Glory*...**

**Ant. 2 Those who give to the
poor will have treasure in
heaven.**

Psalm 112

Happy are they who fear the Most
  High,
who greatly delight in God's
  commands.
Their children will be mighty in
  the land;—

the offspring of the upright will be
  blessed.

Wealth and riches are in their
  homes;
their justice endures forever.
Light rises in the darkness for the
  upright:
God is gracious, merciful and
  just.

It is well for those who are
  generous and lend,
who conduct their affairs with
  justice.
The upright will never be moved;
they will be remembered forever.

They have no fear of evil tidings;
their hearts are firm, trusting in
  God.
With steadfast hearts, they will
  not fear;
they will withstand all deception.

Open-handed, they give to the
  poor;
their justice endures forever.
Their power is exalted in glory.

The wicked see and are angry,
gnash their teeth and melt away;
the desire of the wicked comes to
  nought. **Glory*...**

**Ant. 3 May all who serve you,
give you praise, (alleluia).**
Cant: Rev 19:1, 5-7

Salvation, glory, and power
  belong to you,
your judgments are honest and
  true.

All of us, your servants, sing
  praise to you,—

we worship you reverently, both great and small.

You, our almighty God, are Creator of heaven and earth.—

Let us rejoice and exult, and give you glory.

The wedding feast of the Lamb has begun,
And the bride has made herself ready. **Glory***...

READING

RESPONSORY

Glorious are your works, God of the universe. **—Glorious...**
Nothing can surpass your greatness; **—God...**
Glory to you, Source of all Being, Eternal Word and Holy Spirit.
   —Glorious...

CANTICLE OF MARY

Ant. Blessed are the meek, for they shall inherit the earth.

INTERCESSIONS

O God, you are present to us, yet our minds cannot contain the mystery of your being;
   —let what we know of you in the life and love of Jesus draw us to you in ever deepening faith.
It is difficult to wait with hope for what we think is good and just;
   —increase our faith, and help us to hold fast to our dedication to you.
Let the harvest of our land yield enough for all;
   —banish famine from our world; teach us to share.
Eye has not seen, nor ear heard, what you have prepared for those who love you;
   —let the hundredfold that we seek be only to love you totally with grateful hearts.
Jesus, you prayed that we all might be one;
   —help us to recognize those who differ from us as our sisters and brothers sharing this one earth that you came to save.

PRAYER: O holy God, as evening falls remain with us. Remember our good deeds and forgive our failings. Help us to reflect upon and live according to your covenant of love. Be with our lonely and elderly sisters and brothers in the evening of their lives. May all who long to see you face to face know the comfort of your presence. This we ask in union with Simeon and Anna and all who have gone before us blessing and proclaiming you by the fidelity of their lives. Amen.

MONDAY

MORNING PRAYER

Ant 1   Give success to the work of our hands, O God.
Psalm 90

O God, you have been our shelter
from one generation to the next.
Before the mountains were
   formed,
or the earth or the world brought
   forth,
from everlasting to everlasting
you are God.

You turn us back to dust, and
   say:
"Go back, peoples of the earth!"
For a thousand years in your
   sight
are like yesterday, when it is
   past,
no more than a watch in the
   night.

You sweep us away like a dream,
like grass which is renewed in the
   morning:
in the morning it flowers and is
   renewed;
in the evening it fades and
   withers.

So we are consumed by your
   anger;
by your wrath we are
   overwhelmed.
You set our iniquities before you,
our secret sins in the light of your
   face.—

All our days pass away in your
   anger.
Our years are over like a sigh.
The years of our life are seventy,
or eighty for those who are
   strong;
yet their span is but toil and
   trouble;
they pass swiftly and we are gone.

Who understands the power of
   your anger
and fears the strength of your
   wrath?
Teach us to number our days
that we may gain wisdom of
   heart.

Relent, O God! How long?
Have pity on your servants!
In the morning, fill us with your
   love,
that we may rejoice and be glad
   all our days.
Balance with joy our days of
   affliction,
and the years when we knew
   misfortune.

Let your word be manifest to your
   servants,
your glorious power to their
   children.
Let your favor, O God, be upon
   us:
give success to the work of our
   hands,
give success to the work of our
   hands. **Glory*...**

Ant. 2 You turn darkness into light and make the rough ways smooth!
Cant: Isaiah 42:10–16

Sing to our God a new song,
Sing praise from the ends of the earth!

Let the sea and what fills it resound,
the coastlands and their inhabitants.
Let the desert and its cities cry out,
the villages where Kedar dwells.

Let the inhabitants of Sela exult,
let them shout from the top of the mountains.
Let them give glory to the Most High,
and declare God's praise in the coastlands.

You go forth, O God, like a hero,
like a warrior you stir up your fury;
crying out and shouting aloud,
against the oppression of your poor.

For a long time I held my peace,
I kept still and restrained myself;
now, I will cry like a woman in labor, gasping and panting.

I will lay waste mountains and hills,
and dry up all their herbage;
I will turn the rivers into islands,
and dry up all the streams.

I will lead the blind on their journey,
in a way that they know not,
in unknown paths I will guide them.—

I will turn darkness before them into light,
and rough places into level ground. **Glory*...**

Ant. 3 You are gracious, O God; you call us to be your people.
Psalm 135

We praise your name, O God,
all your servants give praise,
those who stand in your holy house,
in the courts of your house, O God!

We praise you, for you are good.
Sing to your name for you are gracious!
For you have chosen Jacob for yourself,
Israel as your own possession.

For I know that you are great,
that you are high above all gods.
You do whatever you please,
in heaven and on earth,
in the seas and all the deeps.

You summon clouds from the ends of the earth,
make lightning for the rain,
and bring forth wind from your storehouse.

You smote the firstborn of Egypt,
both of human and beast alike.
Signs and wonders you worked
in the midst of the land of Egypt,
against Pharaoh and all his servants.

You smote many nations
and slew mighty rulers,
Sihon, king of the Amorites,
Og, the king of Bashan,
and all the kingdoms of Canaan.
You gave their land as a heritage,
a heritage to your people. **Glory...**

READING

RESPONSORY

All nations rejoice and praise God our creator. —**All...**
Sing with joy to the Most High; —**and praise...**
Glory to you, Source of all Being, Eternal Word and Holy Spirit.
   —**All...**

CANTICLE OF ZECHARIAH

Ant. Come to us this day and set your people free.

INTERCESSIONS

Jesus, you preached a gospel of love and forgiveness;
   —may those who hear your word be freed from unfounded
      guilt and a misguided conscience.
You healed those who could not hear or speak;
   —may we close our ears to falsehood and endeavor to speak
      the truth in love.
We know well how to plan for the things we want;
   —help us to plan as surely for ways to open ourselves to
      your Spirit within us.
O God, mobility is a sign of our times; the whole world is within
our reach;
   —protect us all, and guide those who are responsible for our
      trips on land, sea, and in the air.
You desire our good, and you have compassion on all who suffer;
   —be merciful to those who are in constant pain; comfort and
      sustain them.

PRAYER: O God of life, you bring us to this day and we are
grateful for your gift. Enable us to be and to work for
one another in order that justice may reign, that the
needs of the poor be met, and that the oppressed may
be liberated. We pray this in the name of Jesus who
came that we may be free. Amen.

DAYTIME PRAYER

Ant. 1 Teach me to follow in your steps, that I may be your disciple.
Psalm 119:129–136

Your will is wonderful indeed;
therefore will I obey it.
The unfolding of your words gives
    light;
it imparts wisdom to the simple.

I open my mouth and I sigh
as I yearn for your
    commandments.
Turn to me and be gracious,
treat me as one who loves your
    name.

Keep my steps steady in your
    way,
according to your promise;
let no iniquity rule over me.
Redeem me from human
    oppression,
that I may keep your precepts.

Let your face shine on your
    servant
and teach me your statutes.
My eyes shed streams of tears,
because your law is disobeyed.
    Glory*...

Ant. 2 Blessed are the merciful, mercy shall be theirs.
Psalm 82

God stands in the divine
    assembly;
holding judgment in the midst of
    the gods:

"How long will you judge unjustly
and favor the cause of the
    wicked?
Give justice to the weak and the
    orphan;—

defend the afflicted and the
    needy.
Rescue the weak and the
    destitute;
deliver them from the hand of the
    wicked."

They have neither knowledge nor
    understanding,
they walk about in darkness;
the foundations of the world are
    shaken.

God says, "You are gods,
children of the Most High, all of
    you;
yet, you shall die like human
    beings,
and fall like any of their leaders."

Arise, O God, judge the earth;
for to you belong all the nations.
    Glory*...

Ant. 3 Guide us in your way of peace.
Psalm 120

In my distress, I cry to you,
that you may answer me:
"Deliver my soul from lying lips,
and from a deceitful tongue."
What shall be given you in
    return,
you deceitful tongue?
The warrior's arrows sharpened
and coals, red-hot blazing.

Alas, that I sojourn in Meshech,
dwell among the tents of Kedar!
Too long have I had my dwelling
among those who hate peace.
I am for peace; but when I speak,
    they are for war! **Glory*...**

PRAYER: O God, in your love you have given each of us gifts and talents to serve the common good. Help us to use them generously and lovingly, for we are your children. Free us from the desire to serve only our own interests, and help us to grow in the spirit of love that makes us sisters and brothers. This we ask for the sake of all who are in bondage through our selfishness and that of our governments. Grant us our prayer that your love and peace may reign now and forever. Amen.

EVENING PRAYER

**Ant. 1 Your love, O God,
endures forever.
Psalm 136**

We give thanks to you, for you are good,
for your love endures forever.
We thank you, O God of gods,
for your love endures forever.
We thank you, Creator of the universe,
for your love endures forever.

You alone have done great wonders,
for your love endures forever.
Your wisdom made the heavens,
for your love endures forever.
You spread out the earth upon the waters,
for your love endures forever.

It was you who made the great lights,
for your love endures forever.
the sun to rule over the day,
for your love endures forever.
the moon and the stars to rule over the night,
for your love endures forever.
  Glory*...

**Ant. 2 With outstretched arm
you lead us out of darkness.
II**

The first born of the Egyptians you smote,
for your love endures forever;
and brought Israel out from their midst,
for your love endures forever;
with arm outstretched and power in your hand,
for your love endures forever.

You divided the Red Sea in two,
for your love endures forever;
you made Israel pass through the midst,
for your love endures forever;
you flung Pharaoh and his host in the sea,
for your love endures forever.

You led your people through the desert,
for your love endures forever.
Nations in their greatness you struck,
for your love endures forever.
Rulers in their splendor you slew,
for your love endures forever.

Sihon, king of the Amorites,
for your love endures forever;
and Og, the king of Bashan,
for your love endures forever.

Their land you gave as a heritage,
for your love endures forever;
a heritage to your faithful people,
for your love endures forever.

You remembered us in our
    distress,
for your love endures forever;
and you rescued us from
    oppression,
for your love endures forever.
You give food to all living things,
for your love endures forever.

We give thanks to you, God of
    heaven,
for your love endures forever.
    Glory*...

**Ant. 3 In Christ, God's grace is
    revealed.**
    Cant: Ephesians 1:3–10

Praised be the God
of our Lord Jesus Christ,
who has blessed us in Christ
with every spiritual blessing in
    the heavens.

God chose us in him
before the foundation of the
    world,
that we should be holy
and blameless in God's sight.

We have been predestined
to be God's children through
    Jesus Christ,
such was the purpose of God's
    will,
that all might praise the glorious
    favor
bestowed on us in Christ.

In Christ and through his blood,
we have redemption,
the forgiveness of our sins,
according to the riches of God's
    grace lavished upon us.

For God has made known to us
in all wisdom and insight,
the mystery of the plan set forth
    in Christ.

A plan to be carried out in Christ,
in the fullness of time,
to unite all things in Christ,
things in heaven and things on
    earth. **Glory*...**

READING

RESPONSORY

O God, receive our prayer which is lifted up to you. **—O God,...**
Like the fragrance of incense, **—which is...**
Glory to you, Source of all Being, Eternal Word and Holy Spirit.
    —O God,...

CANTICLE OF MARY

Ant. Blessed are the merciful, for they shall obtain mercy.

INTERCESSIONS

O God, slavery is a reality in our world in many forms;
  —grant us a new consciousness of the equality of all people.
You created a new covenant of peace through your Son, Jesus, yet
we live in fear of one another;
  —show us how to re-seed the world with trust; help us to
    put love where there is no love.
You delight in those who receive your gifts with gratitude;
  —bless all who endeavor to develop their talents; encourage
    and enlighten all students, and keep them in your care.
Jesus, you revealed yourself to a woman of Samaria, an
unwelcoming land;
  —enable world leaders to overcome national rivalries and
    centuries of mutual retaliation.
You gave us the power to bind and to loose;
  —free us from our need to control, and give us the grace to
    free others from our expectations.

PRAYER: O God, as darkness falls, remain with us as our light.
Help us to meet you in the scriptures that we read, in
the bread that we break, and in the neighbor that we
welcome into our hearts. Grant this prayer that your
reign will come, that your will be done in us as it was
in Jesus, now and forever. Amen.

TUESDAY

MORNING PRAYER

**Ant. 1 Look with favor upon us
that we may dwell with you
forever.**

Psalm 101

I sing of fidelity and justice;
to you, O God, I will sing.
I will pay heed to the way that is
blameless.
Oh when will you come to me?

I will walk with integrity of heart
within my house;—

I will not set before my eyes
anything that is base.

I renounce the ways of
wrongdoers;
they shall not adhere to me.
Perverseness of heart shall be far
from me;
I will know nothing of evil.

Those who slander their neighbor
secretly
I will ignore.—

Those of haughty looks and proud
hearts
I will not endure.

I will look with favor on all who
are faithful,
that they may dwell with me;
they who walk in the way that is
blameless
shall minister to me.

No one who practices deceit shall
dwell in my house;
no one who utters lies shall
remain in my presence.

Morning by morning I will
renounce
all the oppression in the land,
uprooting from the city of God all
that is evil. **Glory*...**

**Ant. 2 Look upon us with
compassion, O God, and heal
us.**
**Cant: Daniel 3:26, 27,
29, 34–41**

Blessed are you, and
praiseworthy,
O God of our ancestors,
and glorious forever is your
name.

For you are just in all you have
done;
all your deeds are faultless, all
your ways right,
and all your judgments proper.

For we have sinned and
transgressed
by departing from you,
and we have done every kind of
evil.

For your name's sake, do not
deliver us up forever,
or make void your covenant.

Do not take away your mercy
from us,
for the sake of those beloved by
you:
Sara and Abraham, Rebecca and
Isaac, Rachel and Jacob, your
holy ones,

To whom you promised to
multiply their offspring
like the stars of heaven,
or the sands on the shore of the
sea.

For we are reduced beyond any
other nation,
brought low everywhere in the
world this day because of our
sins.

We have in our day no ruler,
prophet, or leader,
no holocaust, sacrifice, oblation,
or incense,
no place to offer first fruits, to
find favor with you.

But with contrite heart and
humble spirit let us be received;
as though it were holocausts of
rams and bullocks, or
thousands of fat lambs,
so let our sacrifice be in your
presence today as we follow you
unreservedly;
for those who trust in you cannot
be put to shame.

And now we follow you with our
whole heart,
we fear you and we pray to you.
Glory*...

**Ant. 3 O God, you are my
shield. In you I take refuge.**

Psalm 144:1–10

Blessed are you, O God, my rock,
who trains my hands for war,—

and my fingers for battle.

You are my rock and my fortress,
my stronghold and my deliverer,
my shield in whom I take refuge,
You bring peoples under your
  rule.

Who are we that you care for us,
mortal flesh, that you keep us in
  mind?
We, who are merely a breath,
whose days are like a passing
  shadow.

Lower your heavens and come
  down!
Touch the mountains that they
  smoke!—

Flash your lightnings and scatter
  them,
shoot your arrows and put them
  to flight.

Stretch forth your hand from on
  high,
rescue me from the mighty
  waters,
from the hands of alien foes,
whose mouths are filled with lies,
and whose hands are raised in
  perjury.

To you will I sing a new song.
On a ten-stringed harp I will play
to you, who give rulers their
  victory,
who rescue David, your servant.
  Glory*...

READING

RESPONSORY

Answer my plea, O God; I trust in your word. **—Answer...**
Before the first rays of dawn, I come to you. **—I trust...**
Glory to you, Source of all Being, Eternal Word and Holy Spirit.
   —Answer...

CANTICLE OF ZECHARIAH

**Ant. Protect us from the grasp of evil, and lead us not into
   temptation.**

INTERCESSIONS

O God, your love is greater than our guilt;
   —have mercy on those who are sentenced to death.
Too often our faith exists only in our minds and words;
   —awaken us to new and practical ways to enflesh our
       commitment to your will.
Our lives are fragile, and you surround us with men and women
in life-preserving professions;
   —guard and guide our police, fire fighters, rescue workers,
       and all who labor and risk their lives for our safety.

Open our minds to the ways that we are destroying the gifts of the earth;

> —bless again the land and water and all of the life that sustains us.

Jesus, you knew the sweetness of friendship, and you gave new life to those who received you;

> —keep us faithful to you and to one another.

PRAYER: O God, you call us to begin this day in dedication to you. May all who need your help today experience your love and compassion through us and through all who have come to know you. Bless all the children of this world; protect them from abuse. May they come to know their worth and dignity as your children, rightful citizens of this earth. This we ask in union with all the innocent and pure of heart who stand in your presence now and forever. Amen.

DAYTIME PRAYER

Ant. 1 You are true to your promise in which I delight.
Psalm 119:137-144

Just are you, O God,
and right are your judgments.
You have decreed your will in justice
and in all faithfulness.

I am consumed with zeal
because your words are forgotten.
Your promise is tried in the fire,
the delight of your servant.

Though I am weak and despised
I do not forget your precepts.
Your justice is righteous forever,
and your law is true.

Trouble and anguish come upon me,
but your commands are my delight.
The justice of your will is eternal;—

give me understanding that I may live. **Glory*...**

Ant. 2 Listen to the sound of my call, O God, I cry for your help.
Psalm 88

My God, I call for help by day;
I cry out in the night before you.
Let my prayer come into your presence,
incline your ear to my cry!
For my soul is full of troubles,
and my life draws near to the grave.

I am reckoned as one in the tomb;
I have reached the end of my strength,
like one forsaken among the dead,
like the slain that lie in the grave,
like those you no longer remember,—

for they are cut off from your
hand.

You have laid me in the depths of
the tomb,
in the regions dark and deep.
Your anger lies heavy upon me,
you overwhelm me with all your
waves. **Glory*...**

**Ant. 3 Hide not your face from
me, O God, in time of distress.**
II

All my companions now shun me;
to them I am a thing of horror.
I am shut in so that I cannot
escape;
my eye grows dim through
sorrow.

Every day I call upon you;
to you I stretch out my hands.
Do you work wonders for the
dead?
Do phantoms rise up to praise
you?

Is your love declared in the grave,
or your faithfulness in the
bottomless pit?
Are your wonders known in the
darkness,
or your salvation in the land of
forgetfulness?

But I, O God, cry out to you:
in the morning my prayer comes
before you.
Why do you cast me off, O God?
Why hide your face from me?

Afflicted and close to death from
the days of my youth,
I suffer your trials; I am helpless.
Your chastisements swept over
me;
your dread assaults destroy me.

They surround me like a flood all
day long;
they close in upon me together.
Friend and neighbor shun me;
my companions are in darkness.
Glory*...

PRAYER: Loving God, you sent the Holy Spirit to the early
Christians as their source of courage and fidelity. Send
your Spirit to us that we, too, may be witnesses of your
love to all peoples on this earth. We pray especially for
the homeless, the displaced, the nameless, the ignored.
May all come to know your love and care, for you are
both mother and father to us all. Help us to recognize
all as our sisters and brothers. We ask this in union
with Jesus, our friend and brother. Amen.

EVENING PRAYER

Ant. 1 May we remember your covenant in this land of exile.
Psalm 137:1-6

By the waters of Babylon,
we sat down and wept,
when we remembered Zion.
On the willows there we hung up
our harps.

For there our captors required of
us songs,
and our tormentors, mirth,
saying,
"Sing us one of the songs of
Zion!"

How shall we sing God's song in a
foreign land?
If I forget you, Jerusalem,
let my hand wither!

Let my tongue cleave to the roof
of my mouth,
if I do not remember you,
if I do not set Jerusalem above all
my joys! **Glory*...**

Ant. 2 Your name and your word are above all forever.
Psalm 138

I give you thanks with all my
heart;
before the gods I sing your praise;
I bow down before your holy
temple
and give thanks to your name
for your steadfast love and your
faithfulness;
for exalted above all are your
name and your word.

On the day I called, you answered
me;
you increased the strength of my
soul.

All of earth's rulers shall praise
you,
for they have heard the words of
your mouth;
they shall sing of your ways for
great is your glory, O God.
Though you are high, you look on
the lowly,
and the haughty you know from
afar.

Though I walk in the midst of
trouble,
you preserve my life;
you stretch out your hand and
save me.
You will fulfill your purpose for
me;
your steadfast love endures
forever.
Do not forsake the work of your
hands. **Glory*...**

Ant. 3 Salvation and glory belong to our God, (alleluia)!
Cant: Rev 4:11, 5:9, 10, 12

Worthy are you, O God, our God,
to receive glory and honor and
power.

For you have created all things;
by your will they came to be and
were made.

Worthy are you to take the scroll
and to open its seals,
For you were slain, and by your
blood,
you purchased for God
saints of every race and tongue,
of every people and nation.

You have made of them a kindom,
and priests to serve our God,
and they shall reign on the earth.

Worthy is the Lamb who was
  slain
to receive power and riches,—

wisdom and strength,
honor and glory and praise.
  Glory*...

READING

RESPONSORY

In your presence, O God, I will find all my joy.—**In your...**
When I see you face to face; —**I will...**
Glory to you, Source of all Being, Eternal Word and Holy Spirit.
  —In your...

CANTICLE OF MARY

Ant. Blessed are the poor in spirit, the reign of God is theirs.

INTERCESSIONS

O God, you have created us free, but our prisons are full;
  —help us to cultivate an environment that inspires life-
    giving choices.
You have created us to choose the good;
  —bless our children that they may know the good and
    pursue it.
You have created us in your image;
  —give us the joy of radiating your goodness, truth, and
    beauty.
Jesus, you experienced the worst of human weakness;
  —grant heroic courage and strength to those who are
    tortured; erase this horror from our world.
You promised to be with us to the end of the world;
  —let us never lose hope in you, and help us to trust one
    another.

PRAYER: O gracious God, open our hearts and our eyes to the
wonders of your presence among us. May we see the
signs of your beauty within and about us and ever be
in awe of the simple gifts of life. Help us to reach
beyond ourselves and to give thanks for all of your
creation that shares this universe with us: peoples of
every nation, animals of every species, all forms of
vegetation, the planets, stars, and all the elements. We
pray this in union with the incarnate Word of God in

whose image all was created. May you be blessed throughout the ages and for all eternity. Amen.

WEDNESDAY

MORNING PRAYER

Ant 1 I will give thanks to you among the peoples.
Psalm 108

My heart is steadfast, O God, my heart is steadfast!
I will sing and make melody!
Awake, my soul!
Awake, lyre and harp!
I will awake the dawn!

I will give thanks to you among the peoples,
I will sing praises to you among the nations.
For your steadfast love is great above the heavens,
your faithfulness reaches to the clouds.

Be exalted, O God, above the heavens!
Let your glory be over all the earth!
That your beloved may be delivered,
give help with your hand, and answer me!

You have promised in your sanctuary:
"With exultation I will divide up Shechem,
and portion out the Vale of Succoth.
Gilead is mine, and Manasseh;
Ephraim is my helmet;
Judah my scepter.
Moab is my washbasin;
upon Edom I cast my shoe;—

over Philistia I shout in triumph."

Who will bring me to the fortified city?
Who will lead me to Edom?
Have you not rejected us, O God?
You no longer go forth with our armies.
Give us help against this oppression,
for human help is vain!
With you, we shall do valiantly;
it is you who will conquer injustice. **Glory*...**

Ant. 2 Justice and peace will spring forth before all nations.
Cant: Isaiah 61:10–62:5

I will greatly rejoice in you, O God,
in you my soul shall exult;
for you clothe me with garments of salvation,
you cover me with the robe of justice,
like a bridegroom bedecked with a garland,
like a bride adorned with her jewels.

As the earth brings forth its shoots,
and a garden makes its seeds spring up,
so will you make justice and praise
to spring forth before all the nations.

For Zion's sake I will not be
  silent,
for Jerusalem's sake I will not
  rest,
until its vindication shines forth
  like the dawn
and its salvation like a burning
  torch.

Nations shall behold its
  vindication,
and all rulers see its glory;
it shall be called by a new name
which your own mouth will give.
It shall be a crown of beauty,
a royal diadem held in your hand,
  O God.

No more shall they call it
  "Forsaken,"
or its land be termed "Desolate;"
but it shall be called "My delight,"
  and its land "Espoused;"
for you, O God, delight in it,
and take it as a spouse.

For as young lovers are espoused,
so shall its children espouse
  Zion,
and as newlyweds rejoice in each
  other,
so shall you rejoice over Zion.
  Glory*...

**Ant. 3 You set us free, O God,
from the chains that bind us.**

Psalm 146

My soul, give praise to my God!—

READING

RESPONSORY

I will praise the Most High as long
  as I live;
I will sing praises to my God
  while I have being.

Put no trust in sovereigns,
in mortal flesh in whom there is
  no help.
When their breath departs they
  return to the earth;
on that day their plans perish.

Happy are they whose help is the
  Most High,
whose hope is in the Creator of
  all,
who alone made heaven and
  earth,
the seas, and all that is in them;
who keeps faith forever;
who executes justice for the
  oppressed;
who gives food to the hungry.

For you, O God, set prisoners
  free;
you open the eyes of the blind.
You lift up those who are bowed
  down;
you love the upright of heart.
You watch over the sojourners;
uphold the bereaved and the
  orphaned.

O God, you will reign forever and
  ever,
through all generations.
  Glory*...

I will sing your praise, O God, every day of my life. —**I will...**
From sunrise to sunset, —**every day...**

Glory to you, Source of all Being, Eternal Word and Holy Spirit.
—**I will...**

CANTICLE OF ZECHARIAH

Ant. In joy and holiness let us serve God our Savior.

INTERCESSIONS

You invite us to be co-creators with you, O God; work is our
privilege;
  —bless employers with all they need to provide safe and
    satisfying work for people in their service.
You have given us stewardship over the earth;
  —make us all responsible workers in time's "vineyard."
Jesus, you teach us to serve one another and to shun ambitious
pride;
  —help us to realize that our nobility lies in our relationship
    to God, whom you have revealed to us.
You knew loneliness and misunderstanding;
  —comfort and sustain those who have been betrayed or
    abandoned.
You came to serve and not to be served;
  —let all who are elected to leadership rise to the responsibility
    of their office and serve with justice and integrity.

PRAYER: See in us, O God, the face of your Christ, and forgive us
our sins. Help all who must live with the strain of
broken and tense relationships. Give us the courage to
love in spite of loss and the mercy to forgive all who
have injured us in any way. May our work this day
bring us and all the world nearer to the quality of life to
which you call us. Grant this through the intercession
of the Holy Family and of all the families like them that
image your life in the trinity of love. Amen.

DAYTIME PRAYER

**Ant. 1 Day and night I hope in
your words.**
      Psalm 119:145–152

With all my heart, I cry to you;
answer me, O God.—

I cry to you; save me,
that I may observe your will.

I rise before dawn and cry for
  help;
I hope in your words.—

My eyes watch throughout the
　night
meditating on your promises.

Hear my voice in your steadfast
　love;
in your justice preserve my life.
Those who persecute me draw
　near;
they are far from your law.

But you, O God, are near at hand,
all your commands are true.
Long have I known that your will
　endures forever.
　　Glory*...

**Ant. 2 Do good to those who
hate you, bless those who
curse you, pray for those who
abuse you.**
　　　　　Psalm 94

O God, avenging God,
avenging God, appear!
Judge of the earth, arise,
render injustice its deserts!
How long, O God, shall
　oppression,
how long shall oppression exult?

They bluster with arrogant
　speech,
they boast, all the evildoers.
They crush your people, O God,
they afflict the ones you have
　chosen.
They kill the helpless and the
　poor,
and murder the parentless child.
They say: "God does not see;
their God pays no heed!"

Understand, O dullest of people!
Fools, when will you be wise?
Can God who made the ear, not
　hear?—

The one who formed the eye, not
　see?
Will God who chastens nations,
　not punish?
God who imparts knowledge
　knows our thoughts,
knows they are no more than a
　breath.　**Glory*...**

**Ant. 3 Judge not, and you will
not be judged; condemn not
and you will not be
condemned.**
　　　　　II

Happy are those whom you
　chasten,
whom you teach by means of
　your law
to give them respite from days of
　trouble,
until oppression is no more.
You will not abandon your
　people;
you will not forsake your
　heritage;
for justice will return to the
　righteous,
and the upright in heart will
　follow it.

Who will rise against oppression?
Who will stand against injustice?
If you had not been my help,
I would soon dwell in the land of
　silence.

When I think: "My foot is
　slipping,"
your steadfast love upholds me.
When the cares of my heart are
　many,
your consolations cheer my soul.

Can unjust rulers be your
　friends,—

who do injustice under cover of
   law?
They attack the life of the
   helpless,
and condemn the innocent to
   death.

But you have become my
   stronghold,
my God, the rock of my refuge.
Injustice will turn on itself,
and evil will destroy evil.
   Glory*...

PRAYER: Compassionate God, we pause to rest in your
presence. May the work we have begun this day find
fulfillment in you for our good and the good of all
people on this earth. We ask this is in the name of
Jesus who is our way, our truth, and our life. Amen.

EVENING PRAYER

**Ant. 1 Behold, I am with you
always.**
   Psalm 139:1–18, 23–24

O God, you have searched me
   and you know me,
you know when I sit and when I
   stand;
you discern my thoughts from
   afar.
You mark when I walk or lie
   down,
with all my ways you are
   acquainted.

Before a word is on my tongue,
behold, O God, you know the
   whole of it.
Behind and before you besiege
   me,
You lay your hand upon me.
Such knowledge is too wonderful
   for me:
too high, beyond my reach.

O where can I go from your spirit,
or where can I flee from your
   presence?
If I climb to heaven, you are
   there!
If I lie in the grave, you are there!

If I take the wings of the morning
and dwell in the depths of the
   sea,
even there your hand shall lead
   me,
your hand shall hold me fast.

If I say: "Let darkness cover me,
and the light around me be
   night,"
even darkness is not dark to you,
and the night is as bright as the
   day;
for darkness is as light to you.
   Glory*...

**Ant. 2 O God, I praise you for
   the wonder of my being.**
   II

For it was you who formed my
   inmost parts,
knit me together in my mother's
   womb.
I praise you for the wonder of my
   being,
for the wonder of all your works.

Already you knew me well;
my body was not hidden from
   you,—

when I was being made in secret
and molded in the depths of the
earth.

Your eyes beheld my unformed
substance;
in your book they all were
written,
the days that you had formed for
me
when none of them yet were.

How precious to me are your
thoughts!
How vast the sum of them!
If I count them, they are more
than the sand.
When I awake, I am still with you.

Search me, O God, and know my
heart!
O test me and know my thoughts!
See that I follow not the wrong
way,
and lead me in the way of life
eternal. **Glory*...**

**Ant. 3 Christ is the firstborn of
all creation.**
   Cant: Colossians 1:12–20

Let us give thanks to God
for having made us worthy
to share the inheritance of the
saints in light.

God has delivered us
from the power of darkness
and transferred us
into the kindom of God's beloved
Son, Jesus,
in whom we have redemption,
the forgiveness of our sins.

Jesus is the image of the invisible
God,
the first-born of all creation;
in him all things were created,
in heaven and on earth,
things visible and invisible.

All things were created through
him;
all were created for him.
He is before all else that is.
In him all things hold together.

He is the head of the body, the
church!
He is the beginning,
the firstborn from the dead,
that in everything, he might be
above all others.

In him all the fullness of God was
pleased to dwell,
and, through him, to reconcile all
things to himself,
whether on earth or in heaven,
making peace by the blood of his
cross. **Glory*...**

READING

RESPONSORY

Keep us, O God, on the path to life. **—Keep us...**
May your hand ever guide us **—on the path...**
Glory to you, Source of all Being, Eternal Word and Holy Spirit.
   —Keep us...

CANTICLE OF MARY

Ant. Blessed are they who mourn for they shall be comforted.

INTERCESSIONS

Your justice is governed by mercy, O God;
—strengthen those whose work exposes them to temptations
to greed or unjust dealings.
Inspire those who can to give aid to worthy endeavors;
—let their hundredfold be a deepened awareness of your
presence in their lives.
Have mercy on abused spouses and children and on those who
abuse them;
—help us to enable them to begin life anew.
Spirit of God, joy and peace are your gifts to us;
—bless all who lighten our burden by their thoughtfulness,
humor, and creativity.
Jesus, you remind us that we cannot serve two masters;
—give us a single heart that seeks what is good, receiving all
from God with trust.

PRAYER: O God, look upon the poverty of our hearts with
compassion and love. Enable us to give lovingly and
freely of our possessions and gifts. May those who work
with the poor and needy receive joy in this life and
fullness of life forever. This we ask through the
intercession of all the saints, especially of those whose
legacy of service we carry on today. Grant that we may
be faithful as they were faithful, so that we too may live
with you forever. Amen.

THURSDAY

MORNING PRAYER

**Ant. 1 In the early morning, O
God, I remember your
steadfast love.
Psalm 143:1–11**

Hear my prayer, O God;
give ear to my supplication!—

In your justice and faithfulness
answer me!
Do not call your servant to
judgment
for no one is righteous before
you.

For evil pursues my soul,
crushing my life to the ground,
making me dwell in darkness
like the dead, long forgotten.
Therefore my spirit faints within
  me;
my heart within me is appalled.

I remember the days gone before,
I ponder on all you have done;
I muse on what you have
  wrought.
To you I stretch out my hands;
my soul thirsts for you like
  parched land.

O God, make haste to answer me!
My spirit fails within me!
Hide not your face from me,
lest I be like those who go down
  to the grave.

Let me hear in the morning of
  your steadfast love,
for in you I put my trust.
Teach me the way I should go,
for to you I lift up my soul.

Deliver me, O God, from all evil!
I have fled to you for refuge!
Teach me to do your will,
for you are my God!
Let your good spirit lead me
in ways that are level and
  smooth!

For your name's sake, save my
  life!
In your justice bring me out of
  trouble.   **Glory*...**

**Ant. 2 I have sheltered you as a
hen shelters her brood!
    Cant: Isaiah 66:10–14a**

"Rejoice with Jerusalem, and be
glad for her, all you who love
her;—

rejoice with her in joy,
all you who mourn over her;
that you may suck and be
  satisfied with her consoling
  breasts;
that you may drink deeply with
  delight from the abundance of
  her glory."

For thus says God Most High:
"Behold, I will extend prosperity
  to her like a river,
and the wealth of the nations like
  an overflowing stream.

As nurslings, you shall be carried
  upon her hip,
and fondled on her lap.

As a parent comforts a child,
  so will I comfort you;
you shall be comforted in
  Jerusalem.

You shall see, and your hearts
  shall rejoice;
your beings flourish like the
  grass.   **Glory*...**

**Ant. 3 Through you, the blind
see, the lame walk, and the
poor hear the good news.
    Psalm 147:1–11**

It is good to sing praise to you;
for you are gracious and merciful;
to you our praise is due.

You, O God, build up Jerusalem;
you gather the outcasts of Israel.
You heal the broken-hearted,
and bind up their wounds.
You fix the number of the stars,
and give to each its name.

You are great and almighty,
your wisdom beyond all measure.
For you lift up the poor and
  downtrodden,—

you put oppression to rout.

We sing to you with thanksgiving;
make melody upon the lyre!

You cover the heavens with
  clouds,
you prepare rain for the earth,
make mountains sprout with
  grass.
You provide beasts with their
  food,—

and the young ravens that cry.
You delight not in the strength of
  the horse,
nor take pleasure in human
  indulgence;
but you delight in those who
  revere you,
in those who hope in your love.
  Glory*...

READING

RESPONSORY

O God, you have made of us a priesthood, baptized in the blood of
  Christ. **—O God...**
You send us to all nations; **—baptized...**
Glory to you, Source of all Being, Eternal Word and Holy Spirit.
  —O God...

CANTICLE OF ZECHARIAH

**Ant. Send your light and your truth to those who dwell in
  darkness.**

INTERCESSIONS

O God, no one is beyond the reach of your love;
  —help us to appreciate one another as we are, not expecting
    more than we can do or give.
Our culture is heavy with the lure of material gain;
  —deliver us from the temptation to use others for our own
    profit.
Jesus, your Spirit dwells in our hearts;
  —keep us open to the wisdom and gifts of everyone.
Wealthy men and women were among your followers, and they
supported your mission;
  —show us how to use whatever we have in keeping with your
    gospel.
We have walked on the moon, and technology reaches deeper and
deeper into the galaxies;
  —may scientific research deepen our thirst for the wisdom and
    knowledge of God.

PRAYER: O God, you call us to be your people and to minister to one another. Look with pity on all who are held captive by the bonds of addiction. Free us from our own destructive impulses that we may choose life and enable others to find what is life-giving for them. Give discernment and wisdom to all who minister to those seeking liberation from any forms of addiction, that we may all know the joy of the freedom that is ours as your children. This we ask of you, who are our Mother, our Father, our Guardian, our God, Creator and Preserver of us all, both now and in eternity. Amen.

DAYTIME PRAYER

Ant. 1 Give me life according to your justice.

Psalm 119:153–160

Look on my affliction and deliver
　me,
for I remember your law.
Plead my cause and redeem me;
give me life according to your
　promise!

Salvation is far from the wicked,
for they do not seek your
　statutes.
Great is your mercy, O God;
give me life according to your
　justice.

Though my foes and oppressors
　are many,
I have not swerved from your will.
I look at evil with disgust,
because it seeks to snare me.

See how I love your precepts!
Preserve my life in your love.
The whole of your word is truth;
your decrees are eternal.
　Glory*...

Ant. 2 Bless the work of our hands, O God.

Psalm 128

Blessed are they who fear you, O
　God,
and walk in your ways!

By the labor of their hands they
　shall eat.
A husband will be happy and
　prosper;
a wife like a fruitful vine
　in the heart of her house;
their children like olive shoots
　around their table.

Indeed thus shall be blessed
those who fear you, O God.

May you bless them from Zion
all the days of their lives!
May they see their children's
　children in a happy Jerusalem!
　Glory*...

Ant. 3 Deliver me for the sake of your love.

Psalm 6

O God, rebuke me not for my
  frailties,
nor chastise me in my weakness.
Be gracious to me for I am
  languishing;
heal me, for my bones are
  troubled.
My soul is sorely troubled.
But you, O God—how long?

Turn, O God, save my life;
deliver me for the sake of your
  love.
For in death there is no
  remembrance of you;—

in the grave who can give you
  praise?

I am weary with my moaning;
every night I flood my bed with
  tears;
I drench my couch with my
  weeping.
My eyes waste away because of
  my grief,
they grow weak because of my
  misfortune.

Let this darkness depart from me;
hear the sound of my weeping.
You will hear my supplication;
you will accept my prayer.
  Glory*...

PRAYER: Bountiful God, you nourish us daily with the bread of life and the bread that is the work of our hands. May all the peoples and creatures of this earth have the nourishment they need to live their lives fully. Help us to solve the problems of food distribution, drought, expanding deserts, malnutrition, famine, and disease, that all may share in the banquet and none will be in want. We ask this through Jesus, our Bread of Life. Amen.

EVENING PRAYER

Ant. 1 I will sing a new song to you, for you are my refuge.

Psalm 144:1-10

Blessed are you, O God, my rock,
who train mÿ hands for war,
and my fingers for battle.

You are my rock and my fortress,
my stronghold and my deliverer,
my shield in whom I take refuge,
You bring peoples under your
  rule.

Who are we that you care for us,
mortal flesh, that you keep us in
  mind?
We, who are merely a breath,
whose days are like a passing
  shadow.

Lower your heavens and come
  down!
Touch the mountains that they
  smoke!
Flash your lightnings and scatter
  them,—

shoot your arrows and put them
  to flight.

Stretch forth your hand from on
  high,
rescue me from the mighty
  waters,
from the hands of alien foes,
whose mouths are filled with lies,
and whose hands are raised in
  perjury.

To you will I sing a new song.
On a ten-stringed harp I will play
to you, who give rulers their
  victory,
who rescue David, your servant.
  Glory*...

**Ant. 2 Happy are the people
whose God is our God.**
          II

To you I will sing a new song;
I will play on the ten-stringed
  harp,
to you who give rulers their
  victory,
who set David your servant free.

You set him free from the evil
  sword,
and delivered him from alien foes,
whose mouths were filled with
  lies,
whose hands were raised in
  perjury.

Let our sons in their youth be like
  plants full grown,
our daughters like graceful
  columns
adorned as though for a palace.

Let our granaries be full, with
  crops of every kind;
may our sheep bring forth
  thousands—

and ten thousands in our fields;
may our cattle be heavy with
  young,
suffering no mischance in
  bearing.

May there be no ruined wall, no
  exile,
no cry of distress in our streets.
Happy the people with such
  blessings!
Happy the people whose God is
  our God.   **Glory*...**

**Ant. 3 Now is the time of
salvation for those who revere
your name.**
       **Cant: Rev 11: 17–18;
          12:10b–12a**

We give thanks to you, God
  Almighty,
who is and who was.
You have assumed your great
  power,
you have begun your reign.

The nations raged, but your
  wrath came,
and the time for the dead to be
  judged,
for rewarding your servants, the
  prophets and saints,
and those who revere your name,
the great and small alike.

Now the salvation, the power and
  the reign have come,
of God and of the Christ,
for the accusers of our loved ones
  have been thrown down,
who accuse them day and night.

They have been conquered by the
  blood of the Lamb,
and by the word of their
  testimony,—

for love of life did not deter them
from death.
Rejoice then, O heavens,—

and you that dwell therein!
Glory*...

READING

RESPONSORY

You bless the peacemakers, and call them your children.
—You bless...
You give them your spirit, **—and call...**
Glory to you, Source of all Being, Eternal Word and Holy Spirit.
—You bless...

CANTICLE OF MARY

Ant. Blessed are the peacemakers, for they shall be called children of God.

INTERCESSIONS

O God, creator of all that is;
—bless the work of our hands.
Jesus, revelation of God to us;
—teach us to speak and live the truth.
Holy Spirit, dwelling in our hearts;
—deepen our love for God and for one another.
Triune God, Eternal Love;
—bless our families, communities, and the nations of the
world.
Holy God, Holy Available One;
—never let us be separated from you.

PRAYER: God of the nations, look upon the lands devastated by war and show us the way to peace. Turn our guns into plows and our bombs into bread. Remove hatred from our hearts and vengeance from our memories. Give us the wisdom and the will to end terrorism and war whether in lands far or near, or in the confines of our families and communities. Help us to remember that we are one world and one family. Grant this through the intercession of all the peacemakers of all times and all places, especially those who suffered persecution and death for the sake of justice and peace. Amen.

FRIDAY

MORNING PRAYER

**Ant 1 Remember me, O God,
make yourself known in time
of affliction.**
Psalm 51

Have mercy on me, O God,
according to your steadfast love;
in your abundant mercy blot out
   my sins.
Wash me thoroughly from my
   offenses,
and cleanse me from my sin!

For I know my offenses,
and my sin is ever before me.
Against you, you alone, have I
   sinned,
and done what is evil in your
   sight,
so you are justified in your
   sentence
and blameless in your judgment.
Behold, I was brought forth in a
   sinful world.

For you desire truth in my
   innermost being;
teach me wisdom in the depths of
   my heart.
O purify me, and I shall be clean;
O wash me, I shall be whiter than
   snow.
Fill me with joy and gladness;
let the bones you have broken
   rejoice.
Hide your face from my guilt,
and blot out all my offenses.

Create in me a clean heart,
put a steadfast spirit within me.
Cast me not from your presence,
take not your spirit from me.—

Give me again the joy of your
   salvation,
with a willing spirit uphold me.

Then I will teach transgressors
   your ways
and sinners will return to you.
Deliver me from death,
O God of my salvation,
and my tongue will sing out your
   saving help.

Open my lips and my mouth will
   sing your praises.
For you take no delight in
   sacrifice;
were I to give a burnt offering,
you would not be pleased.
A broken spirit you accept;
a contrite heart, you will not
   despise.

In your goodness, show favor to
   Zion;
rebuild the walls of Jerusalem.
Then you will delight in just
   sacrifices,
in gifts offered on your altar.
   Glory*...

**Ant. 2 Your love and your
kindness extend to all the
nations of the earth.**
   Cant: Tobit 13:8–11, 13–15

Let all speak of your majesty, O
   God,
and sing your praises in
   Jerusalem.

O Jerusalem, holy city,
God scourged you for the works
   of your hands,—

but will again pity the children of
the righteous.

Praise the goodness of God,
and bless the Sovereign of the
ages,
so that the holy tent may be
rebuilt in you with joy.

May God gladden within you all
who were captives;
cherishing within you all who
were ravaged
for all generations to come.

A bright light will shine to all
parts of the earth;
many nations shall come to you
from afar,
and the inhabitants of all the
limits of the earth,
drawn to you by the name of the
Most High God,
bearing in their hands their gifts
for the Almighty.

Every generation shall give joyful
praise to you,
and shall call you the chosen
one,
through all ages forever.

Go, then, rejoice over the children
of the righteous,
who shall all be gathered together
and shall bless the God of the
ages.

Happy are those who love you,
and happy those who rejoice in
your prosperity.
Happy are they who shall grieve
over you,
over all your chastisements,
for they shall rejoice in you—

as they behold your joy forever.

My spirit blesses you, my God.
Glory*...

**Ant. 3 You feed us with the
finest wheat.**
Psalm 147:12–20

O praise the Most High,
Jerusalem!
Praise your God, O Zion!

For God strengthens the bars of
your gates,
blessing your children within
you,
establishing peace in your
borders,
feeding you with the finest of
wheat.

You send out your word to the
earth;
your command runs swiftly,
giving snow like wool,
scattering hoarfrost like ashes.

You cast forth your ice like
crumbs;
who can stand before your cold?
You send forth your words, and
melt them;
you make the wind blow, and the
waters flow.

You make your word known to
your people,
your statutes and decrees to
Israel.
You have not dealt thus with any
other nation;
you have not taught them your
decrees. **Glory*...**

READING

RESPONSORY

O God, freedom is your gift to all, whether rich or poor.
   —**O God...**
You care for all peoples of the earth, —**whether...**
Glory to you, Source of all Being, Eternal Word and Holy Spirit.
   —**O God...**

CANTICLE OF ZECHARIAH

Ant. Heal the wounds of our sins and grant us new life.

INTERCESSIONS

O God, you have planted the seed of your word in our lives;
   —let its nourishment be the deciding factor in what we choose
     to see and hear.
Faith as small as a mustard seed is enough for us;
   —give us an appreciation of what we have, living in your
     presence day by day.
We long to be instruments of unity and peace in the world;
   —teach us how to support husbands and wives in their efforts
     to be faithful; show us ways to make our culture supportive.
Jesus, again and again you assured your followers with a
calming, "Fear not!"
   —grant your peace to those who live in fear for their lives or
     dignity, those for whom fear is an abiding reality.
Bless the aging who live alone, with family, or in nursing homes;
   —reveal your love for them through those who care for them.

PRAYER: O God, look with mercy on those who are in prison.
Fill their hearts with courage and peace, and let those
who minister to them do so with justice built on
compassion. Free political prisoners, prisoners of
conscience, and all those who are imprisoned unjustly.
Grant this through Jesus who was unjustly condemned
but now lives and reigns with you forever and ever.
Amen.

DAYTIME PRAYER

Ant. 1 Your word is my treasure, O God.
Psalm 119:161–168

Rulers oppress me without cause,
but my heart stands in awe of
your words.
I rejoice in your word
as one who finds great treasure.

I hate and abhor falsehood, but I
love your law.
Seven times a day I praise you for
your just decrees.

Great peace have those who love
your law;
nothing can make them stumble.
I hope for your salvation, O God,
I fulfill your commandments.

My soul obeys your will and loves
it exceedingly.
I obey your precepts and your
will,
for all my ways are before you.
Glory*...

Ant. 2 Let us love one another for love is of God.
Psalm 133

How good and how pleasant it is,
when we live together in unity!

It is like precious oil upon the
head,
running down upon the beard of
Aaron,
running down the collar of his
robes!

It is like the dew of Hermon
which falls on the mountains of
Zion!—

For there God gives us the
blessing,
life for evermore. **Glory*...**

Ant. 3 Guard me, O God, from the snares of darkness.
Psalm 140:1–9, 13–14

Rescue me from evil;
preserve me from violence.
Deliver me from an unclean
heart,
from the chaos of a troubled
mind.
Preserve me from a malicious
tongue,
from sharp and poisonous words.

Guard me, O God, from my
darkness,
and from those who lure me to
evil,
who darken my light with gloom.
Pride and arrogance lay a snare;
greed and covetousness spread a
net;
by my pathway they lie in wait.

I say to you: "You are my God."
Give ear to my supplication!
O God, my strong deliverer,
you shield my head in battle.
Grant not the desires of
darkness;
protect me against its snares.

I know you uphold the afflicted,
you effect justice for the needy.
Surely the just shall give thanks
to your name;
the upright shall dwell in your
presence. **Glory*...**

PRAYER: O God, we remember the agonizing death of Jesus. In
your compassion deliver those who suffer from the

cruelty of others, and heal the minds and hearts of those who inflict pain. Give us a sensitivity to others that is worthy of your children. This we ask through the intercession of all who suffered persecution and death for the sake of others. Amen.

EVENING PRAYER

Ant. 1 Every day I will bless you and praise your name forever.
Psalm 145

I will extol you, O God my God,
and bless your name forever and
ever.

Every day I will bless you,
and praise your name forever.
For you are great and highly to be
praised,
your greatness is unsearchable.

Age to age shall proclaim your
works,
and declare your mighty deeds.
I will ponder your glorious
splendor,
and the wonder of all your works.

Your people will proclaim the
might of your deeds,
and I will declare your greatness.
They will pour forth the fame of
your goodness,
and sing with joy of your justice.

You are gracious and merciful,
slow to anger, abounding in love.
Your compassion extends to all
you have made;
how good you are to all!

All your works shall give you
thanks;
all your friends shall bless you!
They shall speak of the glory of
your creation,—

and declare your marvelous
might,
to make known to the children of
earth the glory of your deeds,
and the glorious splendor of all
you have made.

Yours is an everlasting realm,
and your dominion endures
through all generations.
Glory*...

Ant. 2 You are near to all who call to you with sincere and upright hearts.
II

O God, you are faithful in all your
words,
and gracious in all your deeds.
You uphold all who are falling,
and raise up all who are bowed
down.

The eyes of all creatures look to
you,
to give them their food in due
season.
You open wide your hand,
and satisfy the desires of every
living thing.

You are just in all your ways,
and loving in all your deeds.
You are near to all who call on
you,
who call on you from their hearts.

You fulfill the desires of those
who revere you,
you hear their cries and save
them.
You protect all who love you, O
God;
but evil you will utterly destroy.

Let me speak your praises, O
God,
let all humankind bless your
name forever,
for ages unending. **Glory*...**

**Ant. 3 Your works, O God, are
great and wonderful.**
Cant: Rev 15:3–4

Great and wonderful are your
works,
God the Almighty One!
Just and true are your ways,
Ruler of all the ages!

Who shall refuse you honor,
or the glory due your name?

For you alone are holy,
all nations shall come and
worship in your presence.
Your judgments are clearly seen.
Glory*...

READING

RESPONSORY

Your ways are mysterious, O God, but your love is our light.
   —Your ways...
Your Word became flesh; **—your love...**
Glory to you, Source of all Being, Eternal Word and Holy Spirit.
   —Your ways...

CANTICLE OF MARY

Ant. Guide us in your truth lest we go astray.

INTERCESSIONS

O God, you adorn the earth with the beauty of each season;
   —awaken us to your loving care as you lift up our hearts
   with color and surprise.
You share your life with us through the talents you give us;
   —make us worthy stewards, eager to grow, mindful of our
   use of time.
Your Spirit dwells in our hearts, the very power of your love;
   —let us remember that you are at work in us, never asking
   what is beyond our power.
Lord Jesus, teach us to pray as you taught your apostles;
   —show us how to live quietly and to know how to
   distinguish want from need.

Heart of Jesus, once in agony,
— have pity on the dying.

PRAYER: God, source of all life, have pity on the dying and on
those who mourn. Help them to experience this
transition as a birth to new life; this loss in time as a
realization of eternity. Ease their pain and grant them
your peace which Jesus proclaimed after that first
Good Friday. We ask this in his name. Amen.

SATURDAY

MORNING PRAYER

**Ant. 1 We proclaim your love in
the morning and your
faithfulness at night.**

Psalm 92

It is good to give thanks to you, O
God,
to sing praise to your name, O
Most High,
to proclaim your love in the
morning,
and your faithfulness by night,
to the music of the lute and the
harp,
to the melody of the lyre.

For you make me glad by your
deeds;
at the work of your hands I sing
for joy.
O God, how great are your works!
Your thoughts are very deep!

The foolish ones cannot know
this,
and the dull cannot understand:
though wickedness sprouts like
grass
and evil seems to flourish,
they are doomed to destruction
forever.
But you are forever on high.

You exalt my strength like that of
the ox;
you pour over me fresh oil.
My eyes looked in triumph over
evil,
my ears heard the doom of
oppression.

The just will flourish like the
palm tree
and grow like a cedar of Lebanon.
They are planted in your holy
house,
they flourish in your courts, O
God.
They still bring forth fruit in old
age,
they are ever full of sap and
green,
to show that you are just;
you are my rock, in you is no
injustice. **Glory*...**

**Ant. 2 Give us hearts of flesh, O
God, that we may serve you.
Cant: Ezekiel 36:24–28**

I will take you from the nations,
and gather you from foreign
countries,
and bring you back to your own
land.

I will sprinkle clean water upon
 you
to cleanse you from all your
 impurities,
and from all your idols I will
 cleanse you.

A new heart I will give you,
and a new spirit I will put within
 you;
and I will take out of your body
 the heart of stone
and give you a heart of flesh.

I will put my spirit within you,
and make you live by my
 statutes,
careful to observe my decrees.

You shall dwell in the land which
 I gave to your ancestors;
you shall be my people,
and I will be your God.
 Glory*...

**Ant. 3 Your name is great in all
 the earth.**
Psalm 8

How great is your name, O God,
 in all the earth!

You, whose glory above the
 heavens
is chanted on the lips of babes,
have found a defense against
 your foes,
to silence the cries of the rebels.

When I look at the heavens,
the work of your hands,
the moon and the stars which
 you established;
who are we that you should keep
 us in mind,
mortal flesh that you care for us?

Yet you have made us little less
 than God,
and crowned us with glory and
 honor.
You entrust us with the works of
 your hands;
to care for all your creation.

All sheep and oxen,
and even the beasts of the field,
the birds of the air, and the fish
 of the sea,
whatever passes along the paths
 of the sea.

How great is your name, Creator
 God, in all the earth!   **Glory*...**

READING

RESPONSORY

O God, you are father and mother to us; your love never ceases.
 —O God,...
We have sinned against you; **—your love...**
Glory to you, Source of all Being, Eternal Word and Holy Spirit.
 —O God,...

CANTICLE OF ZECHARIAH

Ant. Fill our days with peace that we may sing your praise.

INTERCESSIONS

O God, time often leaves us longing for more, for we are created
for eternity;
   —help us to find you within, where time and eternity are more
     clearly one.
Your commandments are guides for our way to fullness of life;
   —remind us that law follows life.
Our short lives are a history of your gifts to us;
   —may all that we do give you thanks and praise.
You are ever present to us in our need;
   —let us never be indifferent to the suffering of others.
Spirit of God, our advocate and guide;
   —teach us how to be an effective voice for the powerless.

PRAYER: O God, your love is truth, yet we so often fear you.
You regard us with mercy, yet we see you as judge.
Open our eyes to your goodness and let us realize the
life to which we are called. We ask this through the
intercession of Mary, mother of Jesus, who knew and
proclaimed your goodness to all generations. Amen.

DAYTIME PRAYER

**Ant. 1 I delight in your law;
teach me discernment
according to your will.**

Psalm 119:169–176

Let my cry come before you, O
  God;
give me discernment according to
  your word.
Let my supplication come before
  you;
deliver me as you have promised.

My lips will pour forth praise
because you teach me your
  commands.
My tongue will sing of your
  promise,
for all your commands are just.

Let your hand be ready to help
  me,
for I have chosen your precepts.
I long for your saving help,
and your law is my delight.

Let me live, that I may praise you,
and let your precepts help me.
I have gone astray like a lost
  sheep;
seek your servant, for I do not
  forget your commands.
    Glory*...

**Ant. 2 Listen to my prayer, O
God.**

Psalm 61

Hear my cry, O God,
listen to my prayer;—

from the end of the earth I call,
when my heart is faint.

Set me on the rock that is higher
  than I;
for you are my refuge,
my stronghold against evil.

Let me dwell in your tent forever!
Hide me in the shelter of your
  wings!
For you, O God, have heard my
  vows,
you have given me the heritage
of those who love your name.

May you lengthen the lives of just
  rulers:
may their years cover many
  generations!
May they ever be enthroned
  before you;
bid love and truth watch over
  them.

So will I ever sing your praises,
as I pay my vows day after day.
  Glory*...

**Ant. 3 The needy fly to you for
  refuge.**

Psalm 64

Hear my voice, O God, in my
  complaint;
preserve my life from all that is
  evil,—

hide me from the tempter's snare,
from the scheming wiles of my
  heart.

Evil sharpens its tongue like a
  sword;
aiming bitter words like arrows
shooting from ambush at the
  innocent,
shooting suddenly and without
  fear.

Holding fast to its evil purpose;
conspiring to lay secret snares
thinking: "Who can see us?
Who can search out our crimes?"

But you know well our inmost
  thoughts,
the depth of the heart and mind!
You will shoot your arrow at
  them;
they will be wounded suddenly.
Our own tongues bring us to
  ruin.

Then let all people fear;
they will tell what you have
  wrought,
and ponder what you have done.
The just will rejoice in you, O
  God,
and fly to you for refuge.
Let the upright in heart exult.
  Glory*...

PRAYER: Deliver us, O God, from those who would hurt us and
from our own selfishness. Guard us from all that would
prevent our growth, and let us not be stumbling blocks
to others. We ask this in the name of Jesus who is our
way, our truth and our life. Amen.

INDEX OF PSALMS

	Ps Wk	1997	1998	1999	2000	2001	2002
Sun Cycle		B	C	A	B	C	A
Wkdy Cycle		1	2	1	2	1	2
1-Adv	1	1 Dec 96	30 Nov 97	29 Nov 98	28 Nov 99	3 Dec 00	2 Dec 01
2-Adv	2	8 Dec	7 Dec	6 Dec	5 Dec	10 Dec	9 Dec
3 Adv	3	15 Dec	14 Dec	13 Dec	12 Dec	17 Dec	16 Dec
4 Adv	4	22 Dec	21 Dec	20 Dec	19 Dec	24 Dec	23 Dec
Christmas	Proper	25 Dec	25 Dec	25 Dec	25 Dec	25 Dec	25 Dec
Holy Family	1	29 Dec	28 Dec	27 Dec	26 Dec	31 Dec	30 Dec
Moth.of God	Proper	1 Jan	1 Jan	1 Jan	1 Jan	1 Jan	1 Jan
Epiphany	2	5 Jan	4 Jan	3 Jan	2 Jan	7 Jan	6 Jan
Baptism	1	12 Jan	11 Jan	10 Jan	9 Jan	8 Jan	13 Jan
2-Ord	2	19 Jan	18 Jan	17 Jan	16 Jan	14 Jan	20 Jan
3-Ord	3	26 Jan	25 Jan	24 Jan	23 Jan	21 Jan	27 Jan
4-Ord	4	2 Feb	1 Feb	31 Jan	30 Jan	28 Jan	3 Feb
5-Ord	1	9 Feb	8 Feb	7 Feb	6 Feb	4 Feb	10 Feb
6-Ord	2	–	15 Feb	14 Feb	13 Feb	11 Feb	–
7-Ord	3	–	22 Feb	–	20 Feb	18 Feb	–
8-Ord	4	–	–	–	27 Feb	25 Feb	–
9-Ord	1	–	–	–	5 Mar	–	–
Ash Wed	4	12 Feb	25 Feb	17 Feb	8 Mar	28 Feb	13 Feb
1 Lent	1	16 Feb	1 Mar	21 Feb	12 Mar	4 Mar	17 Feb
2 Lent	2	23 Feb	8 Mar	28 Feb	19 Mar	11 Mar	24 Feb
3 Lent	3	2Mar	15 Mar	7 Mar	26 Mar	18 Mar	3 Mar
4 Lent	4	9 Mar	22 Mar	14 Mar	2 Apr	25 Mar	10 Mar
5 Lent	1	16 Mar	29 Mar	21 Mar	9 Apr	1 Apr	17 Mar
Passion Sun	2	23 Mar	5 Apr	28 Mar	16 Apr	8 Apr	24 Mar
Easter	Proper	30 Mar	12 Apr	4 Apr	23 Apr	15 Apr	31 Mar
2 Easter	2	6 Apr	19 Apr	11 Apr	30 Apr	22 Apr	7 Apr
3 Easter	3	13 Apr	26 Apr	18 Apr	7 May	29 Apr	14 Apr
4 Easter	4	20 Apr	3 May	25 Apr	14 May	6 May	21 Apr
5 Easter	1	27 Apr	10 May	2 May	21 May	13 May	28 Apr
6 Easter	2	4 May	17 May	9 May	28 May	20 May	5 May
Ascension	Proper	8 May	21 May	13 May	1 Jun	24 May	9 May
7 Easter	3	11 May	24 May	16 May	4 Jun	27 May	12 May
Pentecost	Prop	18 May	31 May	23 May	11 Jun	3 Jun	19 May
Trinity Sun	Prop	25 May	7 Jun	30 May	18 Jun	10 Jun	26 May
Corpus Christi	Prop	1 Jun	14 Jun	6 Jun	25 Jun	17 Jun	2 Jun
10-Ord	2	8 Jun	–	–	–	–	9 Jun
11-Ord	3	15 Jun	–	13 Jun	–	–	16 Jun
12-Ord	4	22 Jun	21 Jun	20 Jun	–	24 Jun	23 Jun
13-Ord	1	29 Jun	28 Jun	27 Jun	2 Jul	1 Jul	30 Jun
14-Ord	2	6 Jul	5Jul	4 Jul	9 Jul	8 Jul	7 Jul
15-Ord	3	13 Jul	12 Jul	11 Jul	16 Jul	15 Jul	14 Jul
16-Ord	4	20 Jul	19 Jul	18 Jul	23 Jul	22 Jul	21 Jul
17-Ord	1	27 Jul	26 Jul	25 Jul	30 Jul	29 Jul	28 Jul
18-Ord	2	3 Aug	2 Aug	1 Aug	6 Aug	5 Aug	4 Aug
19-Ord	3	10 Aug	9 Aug	8 Aug	13 Aug	12 Aug	11 Aug
20-Ord	4	17 Agu	16 Aug	15 Aug	20 Aug	19 Aug	18 Aug
21-Ord	1	24 Aug	23 Aug	22 Aug	27 Aug	26 Aug	25 Aug
22-Ord	2	31 Aug	30 Aug	29 Aug	3 Sep	2 Sep	1 Sep
23-Ord	3	7 Sep	6 Sep	5 Sep	10 Sep	9 Sep	8 Sep
24-Ord	4	14 Sep	13 Sep	12 Sep	17 Sep	16 Sep	15 Sep
25-Ord	1	21 Sep	20 Sep	19 Sep	24 Sep	23 Sep	22 Sep
26-Ord	2	28 Sep	27 Sep	26 Sep	1 Oc	30 Sep	29 Sep
27-Ord	3	5 Oct	4Oct	3 Oct	8 Oct	7 Oct	6 Oct
28-Ord	4	12 Oct	11 Oct	10 Oct	15 Oct	14 Oct	13 Oct
29-Ord	1	19 Oct	18 Oct	17 Oct	22 Oct	21 Oct	20 Oct
30-Ord	2	26 Oct	25 Oct	24 Oct	29 Oct	28 Oct	27 Oct
31-Ord	3	2 Nov	–	31 Oct	5 Nov	4 Nov	3 Nov
32-Ord	4	9 Nov	8 Nov	7 Nov	12 Nov	11 Nov	10 Nov
33-Ord	1	16 Nov	15 Nov	14 Nov	19 Nov	18 Nov	17 Nov
34-Ord	2	23 Nov	22 Nov	21 Nov	26 Nov	25 Nov	24 Nov

	Ps Wk	2003	2004	2005	2006	2007	2008
Sun Cycle		B	C	A	B	C	A
Wkdy Cycle		1	2	1	2	1	2
1-Adv	1	1 Dec 02	30 Nov 03	28 Nov 04	27 Nov 05	3 Dec 06	2 Dec 07
2-Adv	2	8 Dec	7 Dec	5 Dec	4 Dec	10 Dec	9 Dec
3 Adv	3	15 Dec	14 Dec	12 Dec	11 Dec	17 Dec	16 Dec
4 Adv	4	22 Dec	21 Dec	19 Dec	18 Dec	24 Dec	23 Dec
Christmas	Proper	25 Dec	25 Dec	25 Dec	25 Dec	25 Dec	25 Dec
Holy Family	1	29 Dec	28 Dec	26 Dec	30 Dec	31 Dec	30 Dec
Moth.of God	Proper	1 Jan	1 Jan	1 Jan	1 Jan	1 Jan	1 Jan
Epiphany	2	5 Jan	4 Jan	2 Jan	8 Jan	7 Jan	6 Jan
Baptism	1	12 Jan	11 Jan	9 Jan	9 Jan	8 Jan	13 Jan
2-Ord	2	19 Jan	18 Jan	16 Jan	15 Jan	14 Jan	20 Jan
3-Ord	3	26 Jan	25 Jan	23 Jan	22 Jan	21 Jan	27 Jan
4-Ord	4	2 Feb	1 Feb	30 Jan	29 Jan	28 Jan	3 Feb
5-Ord	1	9 Feb	8 Feb	6 Feb	5 Feb	4 Feb	–
6-Ord	2	16 Feb	15 Feb	–	12 Feb	11 Feb	–
7-Ord	3	23 Feb	22 Feb	–	19 Feb	18 Feb	–
8-Ord	4	2 Mar	–	–	26 Feb	–	–
9-Ord	1	–	–	–	–	–	1 Jun
Ash Wed	4	5 Mar	25 Feb	9 Feb	1 Mar	21 Feb	6 Feb
1 Lent	1	9 Mar	29 Feb	13 Feb	5 Mar	25 Feb	10 Feb
2 Lent	2	16 Mar	7 Mar	20 Feb	12 Mar	4 Mar	17 Feb
3 Lent	3	23 Mar	14 Mar	27 Feb	19 Mar	11 Mar	24 Feb
4 Lent	4	30 Mar	21 Mar	6 Mar	26 Mar	18 Mar	2 Mar
5 Lent	1	6 Apr	28 Mar	13 Mar	2 Apr	25 Mar	9 Mar
Passion Sun	2	13 Apr	4 Apr	20 Mar	9 Apr	1 Apr	16 Mar
Easter	Proper	20 Apr	11 Apr	27 Mar	16 Apr	8 Apr	23 Mar
2 Easter	2	27 Apr	18 Apr	3 Apr	23 Apr	15 Apr	30 Mar
3 Easter	3	4 May	25 Apr	10 Apr	30 Apr	22 Apr	6 Apr
4 Easter	4	11 May	2 May	17 Apr	7 May	29 Apr	13 Apr
5 Easter	1	18 May	9 May	24 Apr	14 May	6 May	20 Apr
6 Easter	2	25 May	16 May	1 May	21 May	13 May	27 Apr
Ascension	Proper	29 May	20 May	5 May	25 May	17 May	1 May
7 Easter	3	1 Jun	23 May	8 May	28 May	20 May	4 May
Pentecost	Prop	8 Jun	30 May	15 May	4 Jun	27 May	11 May
Trinity Sun	Prop	15 Jun	6 Jun	22 May	11 Jun	3 Jun	18 May
Corpus Christi	Prop	22 Jun	13 Jun	29 May	18 Jun	10 Jun	25 May
10-Ord	2	–	–	5 Jun	–	–	8 Jun
11-Ord	3	–	–	12 Jun	–	17 Jun	15 Jun
12-Ord	4	–	20 Jun	19 Jun	25 Jun	24 Jun	22 Jun
13-Ord	1	29 Jun	27 Jun	26 Jun	2 Jul	1 Jul	29 Jun
14-Ord	2	6 Jul	4 Jul	3 Jul	9 Jul	8 Jul	6 Jul
15-Ord	3	13 Jul	11 Jul	10 Jul	16 Jul	15 Jul	13 Jul
16-Ord	4	20 Jul	18 Jul	17 Jul	23 Jul	22 Jul	20 Jul
17-Ord	1	27 Jul	25 Jul	24 Jul	30 Jul	29 Jul	27 Jul
18-Ord	2	3 Aug	1 Aug	31 Jul	6 Aug	5 Aug	3 Aug
19-Ord	3	10 Aug	8 Aug	7 Aug	13 Aug	12 Aug	10 Aug
20-Ord	4	17 Aug	Assum	14 Aug	20 Aug	19 Aug	17 Aug
21-Ord	1	24 Aug	22 Aug	21 Aug	27 Aug	26 Aug	24 Aug
22-Ord	2	31 Aug	29 Aug	28 Aug	3 Sep	2 Sep	31 Aug
23-Ord	3	7 Sep	5 Sep	4 Sep	10 Sep	9 Sep	7 Sep
24-Ord	4	14 Sep	12 Sep	11 Sep	17 Sep	16 Sep	14 Sep
25-Ord	1	21 Sep	19 Sep	18 Sep	24 Sep	23 Sep	21 Sep
26-Ord	2	28 Sep	26 Sep	25 Sep	1 Oct	30 Sep	28 Sep
27-Ord	3	5 Oct	3 Oct	2 Oct	8 Oct	7 Oct	5 Oct
28-Ord	4	12 Oct	10 Oct	9 Oct	15 Oct	14 Oct	12 Oct
29-Ord	1	19 Oct	17 Oct	16 Oct	22 Oct	21 Oct	19 Oct
30-Ord	2	26 Oct	24 Oct	23 Oct	29 Oct	28 Oct	26 Oct
31-Ord	3	2 Nov	31 Oct	30 Oct	5 Nov	4 Nov	2 Nov
32-Ord	4	9 Nov	7 Nov	6 Nov	12 Nov	11 Nov	9 Nov
33-Ord	1	16 Nov	14 Nov	13 Nov	19 Nov	18 Nov	16 Nov
34-Ord	2	23 Nov	21 Nov	20 Nov	26 Nov	25 Nov	23 Nov

	Ps Wk	2009	2010	2011	2012	2013	2014
Sun Cycle		IB	C	A	B	C	A
Wkdy Cycle		1	2	1	2	1	2
1-Adv	1	30 Nov 08	29 Nov 09	28 Nov 10	27 Nov 11	2 Dec 12	1 Dec 13
2-Adv	2	7 Dec	6 Dec	5 Dec	4 Dec	9 Dec	8 Dec
3 Adv	3	14 Dec	13 Dec	12 Dec	11 Dec	16 Dec	15 Dec
4 Adv	4	21 Dec	20 Dec	19 Dec	18 Dec	23 Dec	22 Dec
Christmas	Proper	25 Dec	25 Dec	25 Dec	25 Dec	25 Dec	25 Dec
Holy Family	1	28 Dec	27 Dec	26 Dec	30 Dec	30 Dec	29 Dec
Moth.of God	Proper	1 Jan	1 Jan	1 Jan	1 Jan	1 Jan	1 Jan
Epiphany	2	4 Jan	3 Jan	2 Jan	8 Jan	6 Jan	5 Jan
Baptism	1	11 Jan	10 Jan	9 Jan	9 Jan	13 Jan	12 Jan
2-Ord	2	18 Jan	17 Jan	16 Jan	15 Jan	20 Jan	19 Jan
3-Ord	3	25 Jan	24 Jan	23 Jan	22 Jan	27 Jan	26 Jan
4-Ord	4	1 Feb	31 Jan	30 Jan	29, Jan	3 Feb	2 Feb
5-Ord	1	8 Feb	7 Feb	6 Feb	5 Feb	10 Feb	9 Feb
6-Ord	2	15 Feb	14 Feb	13 Feb	12 Feb	–	16 Feb
7-Ord	3	22 Feb	–	20 Feb	19 Feb	–	23 Feb
8-Ord	4	–	–	27 Feb	–	–	2 Mar
9-Ord	1	–	–	–	–	–	–
Ash Wed	4	25 Feb	17 Feb	9 Mar	22 Feb	13 Feb	5 Mar
1 Lent	1	1 Mar	21 Feb	13 Mar	26 Feb	17 Feb	9 Mar
2 Lent	2	8 Mar	28 Feb	20 Mar	4 Mar	24 Feb	16 Mar
3 Lent	3	15 Mar	7 Mar	27 Mar	11 Mar	3 Mar	23 Mar
4 Lent	4	22 Mar	14 Mar	3 Apr	18 Mar	10 Mar	30 Mar
5 Lent	1	29 Mar	21 Mar	10 Apr	25 Mar	17 Mar	6 Apr
Passion Sun	2	5 Apr	28 Mar	17 Apr	1 Apr	24 Mar	13 Apr
Easter	Proper	12 Apr	4 Apr	24 Apr	8 Apr	31 Mar	20 Apr
2 Easter	2	19 Apr	11 Apr	1 May	15 Apr	7 Apr	27 Apr
3 Easter	3	26 Apr	18 Apr	8 May	22 Apr	14 Apr	4 May
4 Easter	4	3 May	25 Apr	15 May	29 Apr	21 Apr	11 May
5 Easter	1	10 May	2 May	22 May	6 May	28 Apr	18 May
6 Easter	2	17 May	9 May	29 May	13 May	5 May	25 May
Ascension	Proper	21 May	13 May	2 Jun	17 May	9 May	29 May
7 Easter	3	24 May	16 May	5 Jun	20 May	12 May	1 Jun
Pentecost	Prop	31 May	23 May	12 Jun	27 May	19 May	8 Jun
Trinity Sun	Prop	7 Jun	30 May	19 Jun	3 Jun	26 May	15 Jun
Corpus Christi	Prop	14 Jun	6 Jun	26 Jun	10 Jun	2 Jun	22 Jun
10-Ord	2	–	–	–	–	9 Jun	–
11-Ord	3	–	13 Jun	–	17 Jun	16 Jun	–
12-Ord	4	21 Jun	20 Jun	–	24 Jun	23 Jun	–
13-Ord	1	28 Jun	27 Jun	–	1 Jul	30 Jun	29 Jun
14-Ord	2	5 Jul	4 Jul	3 Jul	8 Jul	7 Jul	6 Jul
15-Ord	3	12 Jul	11 Jul	10 Jul	15 Jul	14 Jul	13 Jul
16-Ord	4	19 Jul	18 Jul	17 Jul	22 Jul	21 Jul	20 Jul
17-Ord	1	26 Jul	25 Jul	24 Jul	29 Jul	28 Jul	27 Jul
18-Ord	2	2 Aug	1 Aug	31 Jul	5 Aug	4 Aug	3 Aug
19-Ord	3	9 Aug	8 Aug	7 Aug	12 Aug	11 Aug	10 Aug
20-Ord	4	16 Aug	15 Aug	14 Aug	19 Aug	18 Aug	17 Aug
21-Ord	1	23 Aug	22 Aug	21 Aug	26 Aug	25 Aug	24 Aug
22-Ord	2	30 Aug	29 Aug	28 Aug	2 Sep	1 Sep	31 Aug
23-Ord	3	6 Sep	5 Sep	4 Sep	9 Sep	8 Sep	7 Sep
24-Ord	4	13 Sep	12 Sep	11 Sep	16 Sep	15 Sep	14 Sep
25-Ord	1	20 Sep	19 Sep	18 Sep	23 Sep	22 Sep	21 Sep
26-Ord	2	27 Sep	26 Sep	25 Sep	30 Sep	29 Sep	28 Sep
27-Ord	3	4 Oct	3 Oct	2 Oct	7 Oct	6 Oct	5 Oct
28-Ord	4	11 Oct	10 Oct	9 Oct	14 Oct	13 Oct	12 Oct
29-Ord	1	18 Oct	17 Oct	16 Oct	21 Oct	20 Oct	19 Oct
30-Ord	2	25 Oct	24 Oct	23 Oct	28 Oct	27 Oct	26 Oct
31-Ord	3	All Saints	31 Oct	30 Oct	4 Nov	3 Nov	2Nov
32-Ord	4	8 Nov	7 Nov	6 Nov	11 Nov	10 Nov	9 Nov
33-Ord	1	15 Nov	14 Nov	13 Nov	18 Nov	17 Nov	16 Nov
34-Ord	2	22 Nov	21 Nov	20 Nov	25 Nov	24 Nov	23 Nov

	Ps Wk	2015	2016	2017	2018	2019	2020
Sun Cycle		B	C	A	B	C	A
Wkdy Cycle		1	2	1	2	1	2
1-Adv	1	30 Nov 14	29 Nov 15	27 Nov 16	3 Dec 17	2 Dec 18	1 Dec 19
2-Adv	2	7 Dec	6 Dec	4 Dec	10 Dec	9 Dec	8 Dec
3 Adv	3	14 Dec	13 Dec	11 Dec	17 Dec	16 Dec	15 Dec
4 Adv	4	21 Dec	20 Dec	18 Dec	24 Dec	23 Dec	22 Dec
Christmas	Proper	25 Dec	25 Dec	25 Dec	25 Dec	25 Dec	25 Dec
Holy Family	1	28 Dec	27 Dec	2 Jan	31 Dec	30 Dec	29 Dec
Moth.of God	Proper	1 Jan	1 Jan	1 Jan	1 Jan	1 Jan	1 Jan
Epiphany	2	4 Jan	3 Jan	8 Jan	7 Jan	6 Jan	5 Jan
Baptism	1	11 Jan	10 Jan	9 Jan	14 Jan	13 Jan	12 Jan
2-Ord	2	18 Jan	17 Jan	15 Jan	21 Jan	20 Jan	19 Jan
3-Ord	3	25 Jan	24 Jan	22 Jan	28 Jan	27 Jan	26 Jan
4-Ord	4	1`Feb	31 Jan	29 Jan	4 Feb	3 Feb	2 Feb
5-Ord	1	8 Feb	7 Feb	–	–	10 Feb	9 Feb
6-Ord	2	15 Feb	–	–	–	17 Feb	16 Feb
7-Ord	3	–	–	5 Feb	–	24 Feb	23 Feb
8-Ord	4	–	–	12 Feb	–	3 Mar	–
9-Ord	1	–	–	19 Feb	–	–	–
Ash Wed	4	18 Feb	10 Feb	26 Feb	14 Feb	6 Mar	22 Feb
1 Lent	1	22 Feb	14 Feb	5 Mar	18 Feb	10 Mar	1 Mar
2 Lent	2	1 Mar	21 Feb	12 Mar	25 Feb	17 Mar	8 Mar
3 Lent	3	8 Mar	28 Feb	19 Mar	4 Mar	24 Mar	15 Mar
4 Lent	4	15 Mar	6 Mar	26 Mar	11 Mar	31 Mar	22 Mar
5 Lent	1	22 Mar	13 Mar	2 Apr	18 Mar	7 Apr	29 Mar
Passion Sun	2	29 Mar	20 Mar	9 Apr	25 Mar	14 Apr	5 Apr
Easter	Proper	5 Apr	27 Mar	16 Apr	1 Apr	21 Apr	12 Apr
2 Easter	2	12 Apr	3 Apr	23 Apr	8 Apr	28 Apr	19 Apr
3 Easter	3	19 Apr	10 Apr	30 Apr	15 Apr	5 May	26 Apr
4 Easter	4	26 Apr	17 Apr	7 May	22 Apr	12 May	3 May
5 Easter	1	3 May	24 Apr	14 May	29 Apr	19 May	10 May
6 Easter	2	10 May	1 May	21 May	6 May	26 May	17 May
Ascension	Proper	17 May	8 May	28 May	13 May	2 June	24 May
7 Easter	3	24 May	15 May	4 Jun	20 May	9 Jun	31 May
Pentecost	Prop	31 May	22 May	11 Jun	27 May	16 Jun	7 Jun
Trinity Sun	Prop	7 Jun	29 May	18 Jun	3 Jun	23 Jun	14 Jun
Corpus Christi	Prop	14 Jun	5 Jun	25 Jun	10 Jun	30 Jun	21 Jun
10-Ord	2	–	–	–	–	–	–
11-Ord	3	–	12 Jun	–	17 Jun	–	–
12-Ord	4	21 Jun	19 Jun	–	24 Jun	–	–
13-Ord	1	28 Jun	26 Jun	2 Jul	1 Jul	–	28 Jun
14-Ord	2	5 Jul	3 Jul	9 Jul	8 Jul	7 Jul	5 Jul
15-Ord	3	12 Jul	10 Jul	16 Jul	15 Jul	14 Jul	12 Jul
16-Ord	4	19 Jul	17 Jul	23 Jul	22 Jul	21 Jul	19 Jul
17-Ord	1	26 Jul	24 Jul	30 Jul	29 Jul	28 Jul	26 Jul
18-Ord	2	2Aug	31 Jul	6 Aug	5 Aug	4 Aug	2 Aug
19-Ord	3	9 Aug	7 Aug	13 Aug	12 Aug	11 Aug	9 Aug
20-Ord	4	16 Aug	14 Aug	20 Aug	19 Aug	18 Aug	16 Aug
21-Ord	1	23 Aug	21 Aug	27 Aug	26 Aug	25 Aug	23 Aug
22-Ord	2	30 Aug	28 Aug	3 Sep	2 Sep	1 Sep	30 Aug
23-Ord	3	6 Sep	4 Sep	10 Sep	9 Sep	8 Sep	6 Sep
24-Ord	4	13 Sep	11 Sep	17 Sep	16 Sep	15 Sep	13 Sep
25-Ord	1	20 Sep	18 Sep	24 Sep	23 Sep	22 Sep	20 Sep
26-Ord	2	27 Sep	25 Sep	1 Oct	30 Sep	29 Sep	27 Sep
27-Ord	3	4 Oct	2 Oct	8 Oct	7 Oct	6 Oct	4 Oct
28-Ord	4	11 Oct	9 Oct	15 Oct	14 Oct	13 Oct	11 Oct
29-Ord	1	18 Oct	16 Oct	22 Oct	21 Oct	20 Oct	18 Oct
30-Ord	2	25 Oct	23 Oct	29 Oct	28 Oct	27 Oct	25 Oct
31-Ord	3	1 Nov	30 Oct	5 Nov	4 Nov	3 Nov	1 Nov
32-Ord	4	8 Nov	6 Nov	12 Nov	11 Nov	10 Nov	8 Nov
33-Ord	1	15 Nov	13 Nov	19 Nov	18 Nov	17 Nov	15 Nov
34-Ord	2	22Nov	20 Nov	26 Nov	25 Nov	24 Nov	22 Nov

CANTICLE OF ZECHARIAH

Blessed are you, God of Israel
for you have visited and redeemed your people,
and have raised up a horn of salvation for us
in the house of your servant.

As you spoke through the mouths
of your holy prophets from of old,
that we should be saved from our enemies,
and from the hand of all who oppress us;

to perform the mercy promised to our ancestors,
and to remember your holy covenant,

the oath you swore to Abraham and Sarah,
to grant us deliverance from evil,
that we might serve you without fear,
in holiness and righteousness
all the days of our lives.

And you, child,
will be called the prophet of the Most High,
for you will go before the Holy One
to prepare God's ways,

to give knowledge of salvation to God's people
in the forgiveness of their sins,

through the tender mercy of our God
when the day shall dawn upon us from on high

to give light to those who sit in darkness
and in the shadow of death,
to guide our feet
into the way of peace.   Glory...